The Eye Single

John Lundell
with C. Menyennett

The Eye Single copyright © 2016 John Lundell
All rights reserved. No part of this book may be reproduced, stored in a retrieval system, or transmitted, in any form, or by any means, electronic, mechanical, photocopying, recording, or otherwise, without written permission of the publisher.
Morning Glory at morningglory.website
Booksite at theeyesingle.com

Originally published as *Watching With Jesus*, copyright 2002
First Edition of illustrated and revised version, *The Eye Single*, 2016
First electronic publication of *The Eye Single*, 2016

Unless otherwise indicated, Scripture quotations used in this book are from the *King James Version of the Bible*.
Scriptures marked ESV are from the *Holy Bible, English Standard Version* (ESV® Bible), copyright © 2001 by Crossway, a publishing ministry of Good News Publishers. Used by permission.
Scriptures marked LITV are from the *Literal Translation of the Holy Bible* (LITV® Bible), copyright © 1993 by Jay P. Green Sr. Used by permission of the copyright holder.
Scriptures marked (YLT) are from *Young's Literal Translation* by Robert Young, published in 1898. Available online and through Baker Book House.
Scriptures marked ASV are from *The Holy Bible: American Standard Version*, copyright © 1901 (expired) by Thomas Nelson & Sons. This translation is the predecessor to the New American Standard Bible.

Photographs and illustrations, cover and book design, copyright © 2016 by C. Menyennett
The fish graphic on p.143 is an inspiration from David Morris
The Apollo 17 image of earth, *Blue Marble* (catalogue photo I.D. AS17-148-22727), on the front and back covers, is courtesy of NASA Johnson Space Center.

ISBN 978-1-943715-02-2 *(paper)*
ISBN 978-1-943715-51-0 *(hardback)*
ISBN 978-1-943715-07-7 *(ebook)*

Printed in the United States of America

I thank Patty for a haven in the wilderness.

⌘

*I thank Christ Jesus our Lord, who hath enabled me,
for that he counted me faithful.*
1 Timothy 1:12

The eye with which I see God is the same eye with which God sees me. —Meister Eckhart[1]

> *We are led to believe a lie*
> *When we see thro' the eye,*
> *Which was born in a night to perish in a night,*
> *When the soul slept in beams of light.*
> *God appears, and God is light,*
> *To those poor souls who dwell in night;*
> *But does a human form display*
> *To those who dwell in realms of day.*
> William Blake[2]

Beer Lahai Roi[a]

*And she called the name of the LORD that spake unto her,
Thou God seest me: for she said,
Have I also here looked after him that seeth me?*
Genesis 16:13

⌘

Beatitude

*Blessed are the pure in heart:
for they shall see God.*
Matthew 5:8

---

[a] "The well of him that liveth and seeth me." Wherefore the well was called Beerlahairoi; behold, it is between Kadesh and Bered.—Genesis 16:14

CONTENTS

INTRODUCTION

AWAKE
- WATCH 2
- A NEW BEGINNING 10
- THE TRUTH OF FAITH 16

FROM DARKNESS TO LIGHT
- THE ALMOND TREE 24
- WRESTLING GOD 28
- ABRAHAM'S SEED 36
- CONSUMING THE FLESH 41
- CLOUD AND FIRE 49
- BREAD FROM HEAVEN 55
- MOUNT SINAI 63
- BUILT BY GOD 74
- THE TABERNACLE AND CHERUBIM 79
- I AM 87
- GOD AS SELF 95
- THE FIERY SERPENT 103
- STANDING STILL IN JORDAN 106
- EMPTY VESSELS 112
- THE DOUBLE PORTION 117
- FIRST ELIJAH, THEN ELISHA 122

Contents

I Know My Redeemer Liveth 127
Comes My Beloved 134

The Bright And Morning Star
The Messenger 144
The Watchman 151
The Kingdom Of God 154

The Quickening Spirit
In The Image of Him 164
Celestial Bodies 173
In My Father's House 177
Neither The Day Nor The Hour 181
Commanding Faith 185

Seeing Into Heaven
Heavenly Things 194
The Son Of Perdition 202
The Struggle With Sleep 205
Living In The Spirit 209
When The Trumpet Sounds Long 211
The Prayer 215

Notes 216

As the face of the moon being always turned towards the sun, reflects its light and glory:[1]

> *We all, with open face beholding*
> *as in a glass the glory of the Lord,*
> *are changed into the same image*
> *from glory to glory, even as*
> *by the Spirit of the Lord.*
> 2 CORINTHIANS 3:18

For the glory of God is a living man, and the life of man is to see God. —ST. IRENAEUS[2]

Introduction

> The light of the body is the eye: if therefore thine eye be single, thy whole body shall be full of light. —Matthew 6:22

THE EYE SINGLE is about watching for and with Jesus. When you watch for Jesus, your eye becomes single, your whole body "full of light." Physically, watching is being alert, attentive and seeing. Spiritually, it is much more. Watching is knowledge of God.

> Watching is being.
> Watching is power.
> Watching is consciousness.
> Watching is communion.
> Watching is seeing God.
> Watching is God seeing you.

The scriptures are replete with references to watching. In watchings, prophets saw visions, Paul received revelations and Jesus, Himself, communed with our Father.

> Verily, verily, I say unto you, The Son can do nothing of himself, but what he seeth the Father do: for what things soever he doeth, these also doth the Son likewise. —John 5:19

Watch for Jesus. When you watch for Jesus, you *see* Jesus, for He is here—now. He came back the moment He left. When He ascended into Spirit, He returned in the Spirit, His presence remains. Watch with Jesus.

> Lo, I am with you always, even unto the end of the world. Amen. —Matthew 28:20

You are in the Spirit when you watch. If you are watching when Jesus returns for you in spirit, you see Him and ascend with Him in spirit to live in the Spirit forevermore.

Join with me in "looking for and hasting unto the coming of the day of God,"[1] "looking for that blessed hope, and the glorious appearing of the great God and our Saviour Jesus Christ."[2] Come, "let us walk in the light of the Lord."[3]

> The sun shall be no more thy light by day; neither for brightness shall the moon give light unto thee: but the LORD shall be unto thee an everlasting light, and thy God thy glory.
> —Isaiah 60:19

John Lundell

*Awake
My Father,
Father,
Awake!
Awake in me—
Thee in I,
I in Thee.
Abba,
Father,
See me.*

Awake thou that sleepest,
and arise from the dead,
and Christ shall shall give thee light.

Ephesians 5:14

AWAKE

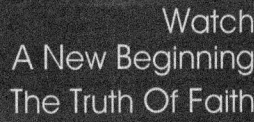
Watch
A New Beginning
The Truth Of Faith

WATCH

THE eyes of the LORD are in every place, beholding the evil and the good.
—Proverbs 15:3

Jesus gave the most succinct commandment in all of Scripture when He said, "*Watch*."

> "*What I say unto you I say unto all, Watch.*"[1]

He instructed his disciples to watch with Him and for Him—with Him while He was here and for Him after He left. He would not be gone long.

> A little while, and ye shall not see me: and again,

a little while, and ye shall see me, because I go to the Father. —John 16:16

Revelation, the final book in Scripture, closes with Jesus saying, "*Surely, I come quickly.*"²

Ever since Jesus ascended, Christians have prayed, "Thy kingdom come, thy will be done." All the while, naysayers have scoffed:

> Where is the promise of his coming? For since the fathers fell asleep, all things continue as they were from the beginning of the creation.
> —2 Peter 3:3-4

The naysayers are wrong. Jesus is here. He came back not long after he left. It was as He said:

> Verily I say unto you, There be some standing here, which shall not taste of death, till they see the Son of man coming in his kingdom.
> —Matthew 16:28

Nathanael was one. Jesus said to him: "*Hereafter ye shall see heaven open, and the angels of God ascending and descending upon the Son of man.*"³

Stephen was another. As he stood before the Sanhedrin, he shouted, "*Behold, I see the heavens opened, and the Son of man standing on the right hand of God.*"⁴

It happened suddenly, "For as the lightning cometh out of the east, and shineth even unto the west; so shall also the coming of the Son of man be."⁵

John saw Jesus in His glorified body:

> When I saw him, I fell at his feet as dead. And he laid his right hand upon me, saying unto me,

> Fear not; I am the first and the last: I am he that liveth, and was dead; and, behold, I am alive for evermore. —Revelation 1:17-18

Jesus had said to Peter, "*If I will that he* [John] *tarry till I come, what is that to thee?*"[6]

Afterwards, a saying circulated among the brethren that John would not die.

> Yet Jesus said not unto him, He shall not die; but, If I will that he tarry till I come, what is that to thee? —John 21:23

Either Jesus has come, or John is still living! John wrote:

> Whosoever abideth in him sinneth not: whosoever sinneth hath not seen him, neither known him.
> —1 John 3:6

Jesus disclosed Himself to Paul. He sent Ananias to tell him of His coming.[7]

> The God of our fathers hath chosen thee, that thou shouldest know his will, and see that Just One, and shouldest hear the voice of his mouth.
> —Acts 22:14

God the Father revealed His Son, the Son of man, to Paul in Arabia.[8]

> But when it pleased God, who separated me from my mother's womb, and called me by his grace, To reveal his Son in me, that I might preach him among the heathen; immediately I conferred not with flesh and blood: Neither

> went I up to Jerusalem to them which were apostles before me; but I went into Arabia, and returned again unto Damascus.
> —Galatians 1:15-17

When Paul, for his own protection, was imprisoned in the Roman barracks in Jerusalem:

> The Lord stood by him, and said, Be of good cheer, Paul: for as thou hast testified of me in Jerusalem, so must thou bear witness also at Rome. —Acts 23:11

Paul saw and heard the risen Savior just as Jesus promised.[9]

> He that hath my commandments, and keepeth them, he it is that loveth me: and he that loveth me shall be loved of my Father, and I will love him, and will manifest myself to him.
> —John 14:21

Jesus returns to rule and reign within you.

> When he was demanded of the Pharisees, when the kingdom of God should come, he answered them and said, The kingdom of God cometh not with observation: Neither shall they say, Lo here! or, lo there! for, behold, the kingdom of God is within you. —Luke 17:20-21

His return is personal.

> If a man love me, he will keep my words: and my Father will love him, and we will come unto him, and make our abode with him. —John 14:23

The Eye Single

A day will come when Jesus will return to rule and reign "without"—over the kingdoms of this world—and we will reign with Him.[10]

> And I appoint unto you a kingdom, as my Father hath appointed unto me; That ye may eat and drink at my table in my kingdom, and sit on thrones judging the twelve tribes of Israel. —Luke 22:29-30

For now, the kingdom is not of this world.

> My kingdom is not of this world: if my kingdom were of this world, then would my servants fight, that I should not be delivered to the Jews: but now is my kingdom not from hence. —John 18:36

It is within. And Israel is a spiritual land with a spiritual city, "which is new Jerusalem."[11]

> Him that overcometh will I make a pillar in the temple of my God, and he shall go no more out: and I will write upon him the name of my God, and the name of the city of my God, which is new Jerusalem, which cometh down out of heaven from my God: and I will write upon him my new name. —Revelation 3:12

Watch For Jesus

> All flesh shall see the salvation of God. —Luke 3:6

Watch for Jesus. Look for the One within you. See Him who sees you.

> Yet a little while, and the world seeth me no more; but ye see me: because I live, ye shall live also. —John 14:19

The moment you look for Jesus, He fills you.

> Behold, I stand at the door, and knock: if any man hear my voice, and open the door, I will come in to him, and will sup with him, and he with me. —Revelation 3:20

He comes in quickly, for He is here already.

> At that day ye shall know that I am in my Father, and ye in me, and I in you. —John 14:20

He comes to "sup" with you, and you with Him.[12]

> As the living Father hath sent me, and I live by the Father: so he that eateth me, even he shall live by me. —John 6:57

Watching for Jesus is watching with Jesus.

> He that seeth me seeth him that sent me. —John 12:45

Look And Listen

> Now it came to pass, as they went, that he entered into a certain village: and a certain woman named Martha received him into her house. And she had a sister called Mary, which also sat at Jesus' feet, and heard his word. But Martha was cumbered about much serving,

The Eye Single

> and came to him, and said, Lord, dost thou not care that my sister hath left me to serve alone? bid her therefore that she help me.
> —Luke 10:38-40

Like Mary, the sister of Martha, sit at Jesus' feet. Look and listen. Choose the "good part." It is the one thing that is needful.

> And Jesus answered and said unto her, Martha, Martha, thou art careful and troubled about many things: But one thing is needful: and Mary hath chosen that good part, which shall not be taken away from her. —Luke 10:41-42

Be Still

Watching is stillness, stillness is grace.

> Be still, and know that I am God. —Psalms 46:10

Still as "a living stone," still as the Rock you worship—say nothing, do nothing, desire nothing. By doing nothing, everything is done for you. Open your eye and you open the door to your soul. In the stillness of watching, Jesus forms within.

> To whom coming, as unto a living stone, disallowed indeed of men, but chosen of God, and precious, Ye also, as lively stones, are built up a spiritual house, an holy priesthood, to offer up spiritual sacrifices, acceptable to God by Jesus Christ. —1 Peter 2:4-5

Be Silent

> The LORD is in his holy temple: let all the earth keep silence before him. —Habakkuk 2:20

Watching is silence, "silence is praise."[13]

> Be silent, all flesh, before Jehovah; for he is waked up out of his holy habitation. —Zechariah 2:13 ASV

You are His holy habitation.

> Know ye not that ye are the temple of God, and that the Spirit of God dwelleth in you?
> —1 Corinthians 3:16

Come, Lord Jesus

> Ye shall not see me, until the time come when ye shall say, Blessed is he that cometh in the name of the Lord. —Luke 13:35

Call on the name of the Lord as you watch, "for whosoever shall call upon the name of the Lord shall be saved."[14] Say or breathe "Jesus, Jesus, Jesus." His name is "a name which is above every name,"[15] and "neither is there salvation in any other: for there is none other name under heaven given among men, whereby we must be saved."[16]

> He which testifieth these things saith, Surely I come quickly. Amen. Even so, come, Lord Jesus.
> —Revelation 22:20

A New Beginning

$\mathcal{A}$ND the LORD God formed man of the dust of the ground, and breathed into his nostrils the breath of life; and man became a living soul. And the LORD God planted a garden eastward in Eden; and there he put the man whom he had formed. —Genesis 2:7-8

When God breathed the breath of life into man, He breathed consciousness. His spirit of self-awareness makes us living souls.

> There is a spirit in man: and the inspiration of the Almighty giveth them understanding.
> —Job 32:8

God, a spiritual being:

> God is a Spirit: and they that worship him must worship him in spirit and in truth.
> —John 4:24

Has a soul:

> Behold my servant, whom I have chosen; my beloved, in whom my soul is well pleased: I will put my spirit upon him, and he shall shew judgment to the Gentiles. —Matthew 12:18

And manifests in the flesh:

> And the Word was made flesh, and dwelt among us, (and we beheld his glory, the glory as of the only begotten of the Father), full of grace and truth. —John 1:14

Man, also a spiritual being, also a soul, abides in God's body of flesh.

> For ye are bought with a price: therefore glorify God in your body, and in your spirit, which are God's. —1 Corinthians 6:20

Flesh is an attribute of Spirit.

> However, "If he set his heart upon man, if he gather unto himself his spirit and his breath; All flesh shall perish together, and man shall turn again unto dust." —Job 34:14-15

The Eye Single

God In The Flesh

> So God created man in his own image, in the image of God created he him; male and female created he them. —Genesis 1:27

"Man" is asleep to God and has been asleep ever since God created "male and female." When God fashioned woman, "God caused a deep sleep to fall upon the man."

> So, the LORD God caused a deep sleep to fall upon the man, and while he slept took one of his ribs and closed up its place with flesh. And the rib that the LORD God had taken from the man he made into a woman, and brought her to the man. Then the man said,
> *"This at last is bone of my bones*
> *And flesh of my flesh;*
> *She shall be called Woman,*
> *Because she was taken out of Man."*
> Therefore a man shall leave his father and his mother and hold fast to his wife, and they shall become one flesh. —Genesis 2:21-24 ESV

Men and women complement and complete each other; we need each other to become whole, to become "Man." In the resurrection we will be complete; in "that world" we will be as before.

> And Jesus answering said unto them, The children of this world marry, and are given in marriage: But they which shall be accounted worthy to obtain that world, and the resurrection from the dead, neither marry, nor are given in

> marriage: Neither can they die any more: for they are equal unto the angels; and are the children of God, being the children of the resurrection. —Luke 20:34-36

God is love and love is relationship. God created man for relationship. He made man His vis-à-vis. He separated Himself from Himself to know Himself. Otherwise, He is simply potential—ideas unexpressed, words not yet spoken, love inarticulate and unrequited—a well of life from which no one drinks. God alone is alone.

Through relationship with man, God wakes in His creation. God in man hears the tree fall in the forest; He feels the ocean spray; He cradles His newborn son.[1] Man, in relationship with God, touches God with his prayers, watching and worship.

Loving relationship is why God formed man and "breathed into his nostrils the breath of life."[2] Shared love is true love. It is love doubled, and doubled again. Love returned knows no limit. It echoes and resonates on and on, forever and ever.

> Beloved, let us love one another: for love is of God; and every one that loveth is born of God, and knoweth God. He that loveth not knoweth not God; for God is love. —1 John 4:7-8

Man lost Godlikeness when woman was separated. God is one; man is divided. Man is two.

> So ought men to love their wives as their own bodies. He that loveth his wife loveth himself. For no man ever yet hated his own flesh; but nourisheth and cherisheth it, even as the Lord the church. —Ephesians 5:28-29

The Eye Single

Man was separated for relationship—one to another, one to God.

> Master, which is the great commandment in the law? Jesus said unto him, Thou shalt love the Lord thy God with all thy heart, and with all thy soul, and with all thy mind. This is the first and great commandment. And the second is like unto it, Thou shalt love they neighbor as thyself. On these two commandments hang all the law and the prophets.—Matthew 22:36-40

Man loves God when he loves His other.[3]

> For we are members of his body, of his flesh, and of his bones. For this cause shall a man leave his father and mother, and shall be joined unto his wife, and they two shall be one flesh. This is a great mystery: but I speak concerning Christ and the church.—Ephesians 5:30-32

It is not until the cross of Christ that man and woman, spirit and soul, are reunited.

> When Jesus therefore saw his mother, and the disciple standing by, whom he loved, he saith unto his mother, Woman, behold thy son! Then saith he to the disciple, Behold thy mother! And from that hour that disciple took her unto his own home.—John 19:26-27

Jesus is the second Adam.[4] Mary is the second Eve, "the mother of all living."[5] She birthed the sons of God when she bore Jesus.

> But as many as received him, to them gave he power to become the sons of God, even to them that believe on his name: Which were born, not of blood, nor of the will of the flesh, nor of the will of man, but of God. —John 1:12-13

If you would know God, behold Jesus. See the One who lives within you.

> For as in Adam all die, even so in Christ shall all be made alive. —1 Corinthians 15:22

The Truth Of Faith

YE shall know the truth, and the truth shall make you free. —John 8:32

Truth is: You are a child of God through Jesus Christ our Lord. God is your Father.

> For ye have not received the spirit of bondage again to fear; but ye have received the Spirit of adoption, whereby we cry, Abba, Father.
> —Romans 8:15

You are a joint heir with Jesus.

> And if children, then heirs; heirs of God, and

> joint-heirs with Christ; if so be that we suffer with him, that we may be also glorified together.
> —Romans 8:17

All things are yours in heaven and earth.

> Whether Paul, or Apollos, or Cephas, or the world, or life, or death, or things present, or things to come; all are yours; And ye are Christ's; and Christ is God's. —1 Corinthians 3:22-23

You are lord of all.

> Now I say, That the heir, as long as he is a child differeth nothing from a servant, though he be lord of all; But is under tutors and governors until the time appointed of the father. Even so we, when we were children, were in bondage under the elements of the world: But when the fulness of the time was come, God sent forth his Son, made of a woman, made under the law, To redeem them that were under the law, that we might receive the adoption of sons. And because ye are sons, God hath sent forth the Spirit of his Son into your hearts, crying, Abba, Father. Wherefore thou art no more a servant, but a son; and if a son, then an heir of God through Christ. —Galatians 4:1-7

You can calm the storms of life.

> And when they had sent away the multitude, they took him even as he was in the ship. And there were also with him other little ships. And there arose a great storm of wind, and the

The Eye Single

> waves beat into the ship, so that it was now full. And he was in the hinder part of the ship, asleep on a pillow: and they awake him, and say unto him, Master, carest thou not that we perish? And he arose, and rebuked the wind, and said unto the sea, Peace, be still. And the wind ceased, and there was a great calm. And he said unto them, Why are ye so fearful? how is it that ye have no faith? And they feared exceedingly, and said one to another, What manner of man is this, that even the wind and the sea obey him?—Mark 4:36-41

"What manner of man is this?"

> Verily, verily, I say unto you, He that believeth on me, the works that I do shall he do also; and greater works than these shall he do; because I go unto my Father.—John 14:12

What do you believe? How deep does your faith go? What does it mean to call God, Father? The Jews knew what it meant:

> Therefore the Jews sought the more to kill him, because he not only had broken the sabbath, but said also that God was his Father, making himself equal with God.—John 5:18

Wake God Within

> Awake, why sleepest thou, O Lord? Arise, cast us not off for ever.—Psalms 44:23

Enter the stark and desolate land.

> He found him in a desert land, and in the waste, a howling wilderness. He encircled him and cared for him; He guarded him as the pupil of His eye. —Deuteronomy 32:10 LITV

Follow Jesus, Paul, the Baptist, Elijah, Moses and Jacob; seek God in the wilderness. Go to the backside of the desert where the bush burns with divine fire. See "eye to eye," and "with open face beholding as in a glass the glory of the Lord," let yourself be "changed into the same image from glory to glory, even as by the Spirit of the Lord."[1]

> Keep me as the apple[2] of the eye, hide me under the shadow of thy wings. —Psalms 17:8

Capture me!
Trouble
Overshadows,
Sorrow
Overwhelms.
Lord,
Here I am.
Where are you?

*Now these things happened
unto them for examples:
and they are written for our admonition,
upon whom the ends of the world are come.*

1 Corinthians 10:11

FROM DARKNESS TO LIGHT

The Almond Tree
Wrestling God
Abraham's Seed
Consuming The Flesh
Cloud And Fire
Bread From Heaven
Mount Sinai
Built By God
The Tabernacle And Cherubim
I AM
God As Self
The Fiery Serpent
Standing Still In Jordan
Empty Vessels
The Double Portion
First Elijah, Then Elisha
I Know My Redeemer Liveth
Comes My Beloved

The Almond Tree

STIR up thyself, and awake to my judgment, even unto my cause, my God and my Lord.
—Psalms 35:23

What follows are tales of transformation and transcendence, stories from scripture that recount the journey from darkness to light. We begin with Jacob, who fled Canaan for Padanaram to escape his brother's wrath.[1] On the way, he stopped at Luz.

> And tarried there all night, because the sun was set; and he took of the stones of that place, and put them for his pillows, and lay down in that place to sleep. And he dreamed, and behold a

> ladder set up on the earth, and the top of it reached to heaven: and behold the angels of God ascending and descending on it. And, behold, the LORD stood above it, and said, I am the LORD God of Abraham thy father, and the God of Isaac: the land whereon thou liest, to thee will I give it, and to thy seed.
> —Genesis 28:11-13

Stone is an image of our eternal, immutable, ineffable God.[a]

> O the depth of the riches both of the wisdom and knowledge of God! how unsearchable are his judgments, and his ways past finding out!—Romans 11:33

To lay your head upon a stone is to rest in the One who never sleeps, the God of dreams. Jesus is the stone. He is "the stone which the builders rejected,"[2] and the Rock from whom the water of life flows.[b]

> Moreover, brethren, I would not that ye should be ignorant, how that all our fathers were under the cloud, and all passed through the sea; And were all baptized unto Moses in the cloud and in the sea; And did all eat the same spiritual meat; And did all drink the same spiritual drink: for they drank of that spiritual Rock that followed them: and that Rock was Christ.—1 Corinthians 10:1-4

---

[a] Jesus Christ the same yesterday, and to day, and for ever.—Hebrews 13:8
[b] But one of the soldiers with a spear pierced his side, and forthwith came there out blood and water.—John 19:34

The Eye Single

Jesus is the silent witness and the ladder to heaven. To rest in Him is to awake in the Spirit.

> And Jacob awaked out of his sleep, and he said, Surely the LORD is in this place; and I knew it not. And he was afraid, and said, How dreadful is this place! this is none other but the house of God, and this is the gate of heaven. And Jacob rose up early in the morning, and took the stone that he had put for his pillows, and set it up for a pillar, and poured oil upon the top of it. And he called the name of that place Bethel: but the name of that city was called Luz at the first.
> —Genesis 28:16-19

The meaning of Bethel is *house of God*,[3] Luz means *almond tree*.[4] The house of God is at the place of the almond tree.[5] The Hebrew word for almond signifies the state of being *wakeful, hastening,* or *watchful*.[6] The almond tree wakes early in the spring to blossom and produce eye-shaped fruit.

> And it came to pass, that on the morrow Moses went into the tabernacle of witness; and, behold, the rod of Aaron for the house of Levi was budded, and brought forth buds, and bloomed blossoms, and yielded almonds.
> —Numbers 17:8

Watchers allow their Creator to form a spiritual body within them. The spiritual body is a house of God, a body of truth and knowledge.

> Lie not one to another, seeing that ye have put off the old man with his deeds; And have put on the

> new man, which is renewed in knowledge
> after the image of him that created him.
> —Colossians 3:9-10

It is a house of love.

> We have known and believed the love that God
> hath to us. God is love; and he that dwelleth in
> love dwelleth in God, and God in him.
> —1 John 4:16

Our triune God, before and apart from creation, is one. He is rock—unchanging, all knowing. But in His creation God changes. He is three—Father, Son and Holy Ghost. Through Jesus the Son, God the Father becomes man by means of His indwelling Holy Spirit. For He will be what He will be.[7] Man, when he watches, returns to his Creator in the Spirit. In the Spirit, he becomes pure, unmoved Being: "*I and my Father are one.*"[8]

Wrestling God

Jacob dwelt twenty years in Padanaram before God told him in a dream to return to Canaan. He returned with wives, children, servants and flocks. When he reached the borders of Canaan, he learned that his brother, Esau, was approaching with four hundred men. His brother had vowed to kill him for stealing his blessing.[1] Afraid and distressed, Jacob sought God.[2]

> And Jacob was left alone; and there wrestled a man with him until the breaking of the day. And when he saw that he prevailed not against him, he touched the hollow of his thigh; and the hollow of Jacob's thigh was out of joint, as he wrestled with him. . . .

"*Let me go, for the day breaketh.*"
And he said, "*I will not let thee go, except thou bless me.*"
And he said unto him, "*What is thy name?*"
And he said, "*Jacob.*"
And he said, "*Thy name shall be called no more Jacob, but Israel: for as a prince hast thou power with God and with men, and hast prevailed.*"
And Jacob asked him, and said, "*Tell me, I pray thee, thy name.*"
And he said, "*Wherefore is it that thou dost ask after my name?*" And he blessed him . . .

> Jacob called the name of the place Peniel: for I have seen God face to face, and my life is preserved. And as he passed over Penuel the sun rose upon him, and he halted upon his thigh. — Genesis 32:24-31

What a startling scripture. Jacob "wrestled a man." God is a man! The One, who walked and talked with Adam in the garden, who supped with Abraham, and who walked through the streets of Sodom,[3] is a man. The One, who made us in His image and whose spirit gives us life, is a man. He is more than omniscience and omnipotence: He is a person, the Divine Person — the radiant sun of consciousness itself — an omnipresent man!

How Can A Man Wrestle God?

Hosea tells us how:

> He took his brother by the heel in the womb, and by his strength he had power with God: Yea, he had power over the angel, and prevailed: he wept, and made supplication unto him.
> —Hosea 12:3-4

Jacob, whose name means *supplanter*,[4] was born gripping the heel of his fraternal twin, Esau.[5] As a young man, Jacob supplanted Esau by first bartering for Esau's birthright and later stealing his blessing.[6] Now Jacob had to face him.

Would God protect him?
He had sinned against Esau.
Was he forgiven?
The Lord had promised to "*deal well with*" him.[7]

Jacob wrestled with all his heart and soul; he wept and pleaded. At first, he did not know who his adversary was. He could not see clearly in the darkness and confusion, but he saw an image. He saw an image that was at least as loving and forgiving, as compassionate and trustworthy, as any moral man. He saw an image of the greatest good. He saw God's image.

> If ye then, being evil, know how to give good gifts unto your children, how much more shall your Father which is in heaven give good things to them that ask him? — Matthew 7:11

Jacob believed, expected and demanded: "*I will not let thee go, except thou bless me.*"

In the glimmering dawn, he saw God's face and became Israel — God's firstborn son.

> And thou shalt say unto Pharaoh, Thus saith the LORD, Israel is my son, even my firstborn: And I say unto thee, Let my son go, that he may serve me: and if thou refuse to let him go, behold, I will slay thy son, even thy firstborn.
> — Exodus 4:22-23

Jacob prevailed and had power with God. The flesh he laid hold of was his own, with its love of ease. He fought off the languor of sleep and held the Spirit in the grip of consciousness all night long.

> Behold, he that keepeth Israel shall neither slumber nor sleep. — Psalms 121:4

Jacob's wrestle with God's image — "a man" — is not unlike your struggle with your God-image. What is He like? What is His will? Will He answer prayer? Will He be merciful?

> How long wilt thou forget me, O LORD? for ever? how long wilt thou hide thy face from me? How long shall I take counsel in my soul, having sorrow in my heart daily? how long shall mine enemy be exalted over me? Consider and hear me, O LORD my God: lighten mine eyes, lest I sleep the sleep of death. — Psalms 13:1-3

God is the creator and sustainer of all flesh and "giveth us richly all things to enjoy."[8] He designed the flesh with all its pleasures; He even "giveth to his beloved one sleep."[9] We wrestle God when we fast and forsake pleasure. We wrestle God when we hold out for a greater blessing.

> Keep mercy and judgment, and wait on thy God continually. — Hosea 12:6

The Sinew That Shrank

During the struggle, when God "saw that he prevailed not against him," God touched the hollow of Jacob's thigh, and Jacob "halted."

> Therefore the children of Israel eat not of the sinew which shrank, which is upon the hollow

> of the thigh, unto this day: because he touched the hollow of Jacob's thigh in the sinew that shrank. —Genesis 32:32

There is only one sinew in the hollow of a man's thigh that shrinks, and that sinew is the compass of man's flesh. Jacob was now Israel—born of God and spiritually alive. A new man, a different man, he no longer walked according to the flesh.

Paul said:

> There is therefore now no condemnation to them which are in Christ Jesus, who walk not after the flesh, but after the Spirit. —Romans 8:1

Jesus said to his disciples and the crowds that followed him:

> There be eunuchs, which have made themselves eunuchs for the kingdom of heaven's sake. He that is able to receive it, let him receive it.
> —Matthew 19:12

How Could God Be Overcome?

How could Jacob prevail? Through prayer and watching. In Scripture, when God gives something to man, man has to pray for it. He gives us the kingdom, but we have to watch for it. Prayer and watching are the hands of faith.

Jacob watched and prayed. He drew God closer and closer until he found Him living within. It was the distant God, the impersonal God—God apart from man—who was overcome. It is the present God, the personal God—God in man—who transcends.

> Men of stature, shall come over unto thee, and they shall be thine: they shall come after thee; in chains they shall come over, and they shall fall

> down unto thee, they shall make supplication unto thee, saying, Surely God is in thee; and there is none else, there is no God. Verily thou art a God that hidest thyself, O God of Israel, the Saviour. — Isaiah 45:14-15

The Face And Faces Of God

After wrestling through the night, God told Jacob to let go.

> Thou canst not see my face: for there shall no man see me, and live. — Exodus 33:20

But Jacob did not let go. He saw God's face and lived. "*I have seen God face to face, and my life is preserved.*"

After he saw God's face, he asked of God, "*Tell me, I pray thee, thy name.*"

God answered, "*Wherefore is it that thou dost ask after my name?*" He had just told Jacob His name — Israel.

God is no longer the life, Jacob; He is the life, Israel. God is man and the Son of man; He is Israel, "and He blessed him there."

Jacob's striving transformed him. He had wrestled his way to Godlikeness; he was conscious in God. Jacob passed away. Behold! Israel lives.

> For ye are dead, and your life is hid with Christ in God. — Colossians 3:3

Jacob is a prefiguration of Christians who "cry day and night unto Him,"[a] who prevail and have power with God and man, and who are the true Israel.

---

[a] And shall not God avenge his own elect, which cry day and night unto him, though he bear long with them? — Luke 18:7

The Eye Single

> He is a Jew, which is one inwardly; and circumcision is that of the heart, in the spirit, and not in the letter; whose praise is not of men, but of God.
> —Romans 2:29

Jacob, Esau And God

When Jacob stole Esau's blessing,[10] he sinned against God. Sin against man is sin against God.

> Against thee, thee only, have I sinned, and done this evil in thy sight: that thou mightest be justified when thou speakest, and be clear when thou judgest.—Psalms 51:4

God, in whose image and likeness we are made, is the inner twin of every man. The very same day Jacob wrestled God, he said upon embracing Esau, "*I have seen thy face, as though I had seen the face of God.*"[11]

> And Jacob went near unto Isaac his father; and he felt him, and said, The voice is Jacob's voice, but the hands are the hands of Esau. And he discerned him not, because his hands were hairy, as his brother Esau's hands: so he blessed him. And he said, Art thou my very son Esau? And he said, I am.—Genesis 27:22-24

Who are you, really?
When you strip yourself of name and title, who are you?
You just are. "I am" is who you are.
The Lord God, I AM,[12] "in whom we live and move and have our being," has as many faces as there are men. "For we are all his offspring."[13]

If a man say, I love God, and hateth his brother, he is a liar: for he that loveth not his brother whom he hath seen, how can he love God whom he hath not seen? —1 John 4:20

ABRAHAM'S SEED

*I*F ye be Christ's, then are ye Abraham's seed, and heirs according to the promise.
—Galatians 3:29

Esau sold man's birthright[1] for a mess of pottage.[2] Adam traded it for the knowledge of good and evil.[3] Jacob (the second twin) and Jesus (the second Adam) strove with God for it. "As it is written, Jacob have I loved, but Esau have I hated."[4]

Jacob wrestled at Peniel; Jesus wrestled in Gethsemane. Jacob wept and pleaded.[5] Jesus cried out in agony. Our Lord was near death[6] as the spirit of man pressed through His flesh.[7]

And there appeared an angel unto him from

> heaven, strengthening him. And being in an agony he prayed more earnestly: and his sweat was as it were great drops of blood falling down to the ground. —Luke 22:43-44

The struggle for the birthright cost them their lives: Jacob figuratively and Jesus actually. Jacob became Israel, God's firstborn son.[8] Jesus, the firstborn of all creation and God's only begotten son,[9] became the first to be born from the dead and the Savior of the world.[10]

> He shall see of the travail of his soul, and shall be satisfied: by his knowledge shall my righteous servant justify many; for he shall bear their iniquities. —Isaiah 53:11

Jesus is our birthright and our blessing. By sacrificing His life for our lives, He obtained our eternal salvation: "For by grace are ye saved through faith; and that not of yourselves: it is the gift of God."[11]

> By faith Abraham, when he was called to go out into a place which he should after receive for an inheritance, obeyed; and he went out, not knowing whither he went. By faith he sojourned in the land of promise, as in a strange country, dwelling in tabernacles with Isaac and Jacob, the heirs with him of the same promise: For he looked for a city which hath foundations, whose builder and maker is God. —Hebrews 11:8-10

God has striven with man ever since his creation, ever since he ate of the tree of the knowledge of good and evil. The Lord God said:

The Eye Single

> Behold, the man is become as one of us, to know good and evil: and now, lest he put forth his hand, and take also of the tree of life, and eat, and live for ever: Therefore the LORD God sent him forth from the garden of Eden, to till the ground from whence he was taken.
> —Genesis 3:22-23

Both Jacob and Jesus suffered sin: Jacob suffered personal sin; Jesus suffered collective sin. In the Garden of Gethsemane, Jesus undid the damage done in the Garden of Eden. He wrestled the spirit enmeshed in flesh.

> For in that he suffered, himself being tempted, he is able to help those who are tempted.
> —Hebrews 2:18 YLT

He opened Himself to the fallen mind of man and engaged the sin and suffering of the world.

> Surely he hath borne our griefs, and carried our sorrows: yet we did esteem him stricken, smitten of God, and afflicted. But he was wounded for our transgressions, he was bruised for our iniquities: the chastisement of our peace was upon him; and with his stripes we are healed.
> —Isaiah 53:4-5

Like a lifeguard who leaps into the maelstrom, Jesus rescued us from the power and consequence of sin. He did it by offering up "prayers and supplications with strong crying and tears."[12] After telling his disciples to watch with Him,[13] He separated Himself from them, fell on His face, and cried:

> *O my Father, if it be possible, let this cup pass from me: nevertheless not as I will, but as thou wilt.*
> —Matthew 26:39

He returned to the disciples, and finding them asleep, said to Peter:

> *What, could ye not watch with me one hour? Watch and pray, that ye enter not into temptation: the spirit indeed is willing, but the flesh is weak.*
> —Matthew 26:40-41

He left them a second time to watch, and prayed:

> *O my Father, if this cup may not pass away from me, except I drink it, thy will be done.* —Matthew 26:42

Returning, he found them sleeping once more.

> *For their eyes were heavy. And he left them, and went away again, and prayed the third time, saying the same words.* —Matthew 26:43-44

When He had finished praying and watching, Jesus came to the three disciples, who had fallen asleep again, and said:

> *Sleep on now, and take your rest: behold, the hour is at hand, and the Son of man is betrayed into the hands of sinners.* —Matthew 26:45

The Son of man was betrayed into the hands of sinners to save sinners.

> *Therefore let us not sleep, as do others; but let us watch and be sober.* —1 Thessalonians 5:6

THE EYE SINGLE

While disciples watch, Jesus prays. He is our advocate, "seeing he ever liveth to make intercession."[14] He prays for us, "for we know not what we should pray for as we ought: but the Spirit itself maketh intercession for us with groanings which cannot be uttered."[15] All we have to do is watch.

Consuming The Flesh

> It was a night of watching by the LORD, to bring them out of the land of Egypt; so this same night is a night of watching kept to the LORD by all the people of Israel throughout their generations. —Exodus 12:42 ESV

Following Joseph's rise to power, the Israelites settled in Egypt and remained there for over four hundred years.

Joseph

Joseph's life foreshadowed the life of Jesus. He became a

servant in Egypt that God might, through him, save His people. Jesus, "being in the form of God," took upon Himself the "form of a servant" that the Father might, through Him, save us.[1] Joseph was cast into a pit and sold to slavers;[2] Jesus descended to earth and was sold to sinners. Joseph governed men in prison;[3] Jesus preached to spirits in prison.[4] The power of God delivered both men. Joseph ruled under the Pharaoh, Jesus rules by the Father.[5]

> And Jesus came and spake unto them, saying,
> All power is given unto me in heaven and in
> earth. —Matthew 28:18

After his death, Joseph's bones were carried away;[6] Jesus' bones were resurrected. Bones are a symbol of the spirit since both remain after the flesh passes away. The taking of Joseph's bones up and out of Egypt prefigures both the ascension of Jesus and the rapture of man's spirit into the Spirit of God.

> And if I go and prepare a place for you, I will
> come again, and receive you unto myself; that
> where I am, there ye may be also. —John 14:3

As long as Joseph was remembered in Egypt, the Israelites flourished. When he was forgotten, they suffered.[7]

> That which fell among thorns are they, which,
> when they have heard, go forth, and are choked
> with cares and riches and pleasures of this life,
> and bring no fruit to perfection. —Luke 8:14

Out Of Egypt I Have Called You[8]

To free themselves from the bondage of Egypt, each Israelite household had to sacrifice a lamb.[9]

> Your lamb shall be without blemish, a male of the first year: ye shall take it out from the sheep, or from the goats: And ye shall keep it up until the fourteenth day of the same month: and the whole assembly of the congregation of Israel shall kill it in the evening. And they shall take of the blood, and strike it on the two side posts and on the upper door post of the houses, wherein they shall eat it. And they shall eat the flesh in that night, roast with fire, and unleavened bread; and with bitter herbs they shall eat it. Eat not of it raw, nor sodden at all with water, but roast with fire; his head with his legs, and with the purtenance thereof. And ye shall let nothing of it remain until the morning; and that which remaineth of it until the morning ye shall burn with fire. And thus shall ye eat it; with your loins girded, your shoes on your feet, and your staff in your hand; and ye shall eat it in haste: it is the LORD's passover.—Exodus 12:5-11

The sacrifice of the unblemished lamb anticipates the sacrificial death of Jesus, the Lamb of God,[a] who became sin for us:

> We were reconciled to God by the death of his Son, much more, being reconciled, we shall be saved by his life.—Romans 5:10

Jesus' blood was shed that it might flow in us.

> Whoso eateth my flesh, and drinketh my blood,

---

[a] The next day John seeth Jesus coming unto him, and saith, Behold the Lamb of God, which taketh away the sin of the world.—John 1:29

> hath eternal life; and I will raise him up at the
> last day. —John 6:54

The blood of the cross colors the doorway to your soul. His death is your death. Your flesh must be sacrificed too: "If any man will come after me, let him deny himself, and take up his cross daily, and follow me."[10]

> And they that are Christ's have crucified the
> flesh with the affections and lusts.
> —Galatians 5:24

Fire roasts flesh; light transforms consciousness. When you feast on the Lamb, you embody the Lamb. The eaten and the eater are one.

> He that eateth my flesh, and drinketh my blood,
> dwelleth in me, and I in him. —John 6:56

The lamb was eaten whole, any uneaten flesh burned.

> If any man's work shall be burned, he shall
> suffer loss: but he himself shall be saved; yet so
> as by fire. —1 Corinthians 3:15

The lamb was eaten with unleavened bread and bitter herbs. Leaven ferments, causing decay, and mirrors sin. Jesus gave unleavened bread to His disciples at the last supper saying: "Take, eat: this is my body, which is broken for you: this do in remembrance of me."[11]

> Purge out therefore the old leaven, that ye may
> be a new lump, as ye are unleavened. For even
> Christ our passover is sacrificed for us: Therefore

> let us keep the feast, not with old leaven, neither with the leaven of malice and wickedness; but with the unleavened bread of sincerity and truth.
> —1 Corinthians 5:7-8

The bitter herbs are the pains of repentance, which is necessary, "for if we would judge ourselves, we should not be judged."[12]

> The sacrifices of God are a broken spirit: a broken and a contrite heart, O God, thou wilt not despise.
> —Psalms 51:17

The meal was eaten in readiness and expectation of the coming of the Lord, with loins girded, shoes on, and staff in hand.

> For I will pass through the land of Egypt this night, and will smite all the firstborn in the land of Egypt, both man and beast; and against all the gods of Egypt I will execute judgment: I am the LORD. And the blood shall be to you for a token upon the houses where ye are: and when I see the blood, I will pass over you, and the plague shall not be upon you to destroy you, when I smite the land of Egypt.
> —Exodus 12:12-13

Firstborn And Second Born

There were two houses, Egyptian and Israelite; there are two bodies, flesh and spirit. God said:

> All the firstborn of the children of Israel are mine, both man and beast: on the day that I smote every firstborn in the land of Egypt I sanctified them for myself. —Numbers 8:17

The Eye Single

The firstborn (the flesh man) must die that the second born (the spirit man) may live. The firstborn must be sacrificed because all must be born again.

> Verily, verily, I say unto thee, Except a man be born again, he cannot see the kingdom of God.
> —John 3:3

Paul wrote:

> The first man Adam was made a living soul; the last Adam was made a quickening spirit. Howbeit that was not first which is spiritual, but that which is natural; and afterward that which is spiritual. The first man is of the earth, earthy: the second man is the Lord from heaven. As is the earthy, such are they also that are earthy: and as is the heavenly, such are they also that are heavenly. And as we have borne the image of the earthy, we shall also bear the image of the heavenly. Now this I say, brethren, that flesh and blood cannot inherit the kingdom of God; neither doth corruption inherit incorruption. —1 Corinthians 15:45-50

If you are watching when Jesus comes, the flesh dies, the spirit lives, and you are caught up on eagles' wings.

God said, "*Ye have seen what I did unto the Egyptians, and how I bare you on eagles' wings.*"[13]

> Wherefore if they shall say unto you, Behold, he is in the desert; go not forth: behold, he is in the secret chambers; believe it not. For as the lightning cometh out of the east, and shineth

> even unto the west; so shall also the coming of the Son of man be. For wheresoever the carcase is, there will the eagles be gathered together.
> —Matthew 24:26-28

If you are not watching when Jesus comes, you are not in the Spirit. You are not in the house drenched with the blood of the lamb, and the Lord suffers "the destroyer to come in unto your houses to smite you."[b]

> The Lord of that servant shall come in a day when he looketh not for him, and in an hour that he is not aware of, and shall cut him asunder, and appoint him his portion with the hypocrites: there shall be weeping and gnashing of teeth.
> —Matthew 24:50-51

To be free of Egypt, you must watch the whole nightlong.

> Watch ye therefore: for ye know not when the master of the house cometh, at even, or at midnight, or at the cockcrowing, or in the morning: Lest coming suddenly he find you sleeping.
> —Mark 13:35-36

The night of the last Passover, the night the Lamb of God offered His flesh to deliver us from the bondage of sin,[c] was also a night of watching. Jesus said to Peter, James, and John:

---

[b] For the LORD will pass through to smite the Egyptians; and when he seeth the blood upon the lintel, and on the two side posts, the LORD will pass over the door, and will not suffer the destroyer to come in unto your houses to smite you.
—Exodus 12:2

[c] For we know that the law is spiritual: but I am carnal, sold under sin.
—Romans 7:14

THE EYE SINGLE

My soul is exceeding sorrowful unto death: tarry ye here, and watch. —Mark 14:34

Cloud And Fire

THE LORD went before them by day in a pillar of a cloud, to lead them the way; and by night in a pillar of fire, to give them light; to go by day and night: He took not away the pillar of the cloud by day, nor the pillar of fire by night, from before the people.
—Exodus 13:21-22

The Israelites watched the Lord day and night. When He moved, they followed. The forces of the flesh followed too.[1]

But the Egyptians pursued after them, all the

> horses and chariots of Pharaoh, and his horsemen, and his army, and overtook them encamping by the sea, beside Pihahiroth, before Baalzephon. And when Pharaoh drew nigh, the children of Israel lifted up their eyes, and, behold, the Egyptians marched after them; and they were sore afraid: and the children of Israel cried out unto the LORD. And they said unto Moses, Because there were no graves in Egypt, hast thou taken us away to die in the wilderness? wherefore hast thou dealt thus with us, to carry us forth out of Egypt? Is not this the word that we did tell thee in Egypt, saying, Let us alone, that we may serve the Egyptians? For it had been better for us to serve the Egyptians, than that we should die in the wilderness.
> —Exodus 14:9-12

The wilderness of watching is death to the flesh man. He will offer every possible distraction and try any temptation to avoid it, anything but stillness and seeing the salvation of the Lord.

> For the flesh lusteth against the Spirit, and the Spirit against the flesh: and these are contrary the one to the other: so that ye cannot do the things that ye would. —Galatians 5:17

Watch, and the Lord watches with you, for He "is in the midst of thee: thou shalt not see evil any more."[2]

> And Moses said unto the people, Fear ye not, stand still, and see the salvation of the LORD, which he will shew to you to day: for the Egyptians whom ye have seen to day, ye shall

> see them again no more for ever. The LORD shall fight for you, and ye shall hold your peace.
> —Exodus 14:13-14

Could it be more explicit? "**Stand still**, and **see** the salvation of the LORD." "The LORD shall fight for you, and ye shall **hold your peace**."

The Crossing

> And the LORD said unto Moses, Wherefore criest thou unto me? speak unto the children of Israel, that they go forward: But lift thou up thy rod, and stretch out thine hand over the sea, and divide it: and the children of Israel shall go on dry ground through the midst of the sea.—Exodus 14:15-16

When Moses lifted up his rod and stretched forth his hand, all the children of Israel watched in expectation. They watched to see the power of God. They watched as before when Moses used the rod of God to bring plague after plague upon the Egyptians. We will also see the power of God if we will only watch, for we are priests, and the priests of God have the almond rod of wakefulness and watching.

> Ye are a chosen generation, a royal priesthood, an holy nation, a peculiar people; that ye should shew forth the praises of him who hath called you out of darkness into his marvellous light.
> —1 Peter 2:9

Watch to part the sea of life. Watch with Jesus, our rod of God. Watch in the power of His Spirit; watch to pass through pure Being. Pass from flesh to spirit on the firm ground of consciousness.

> Behold, I will harden the hearts of the Egyptians, and they shall follow them: and I will get me honour upon Pharaoh, and upon all his host, upon his chariots, and upon his horsemen. And the Egyptians shall know that I am the LORD, when I have gotten me honour upon Pharaoh, upon his chariots, and upon his horsemen.
> —Exodus 14:17-18

We watch to know the Lord, we watch to know I AM.[3]

> And the angel of God, which went before the camp of Israel, removed and went behind them; and the pillar of the cloud went from before their face, and stood behind them: And it came between the camp of the Egyptians and the camp of Israel; and it was a cloud and darkness to them, but it gave light by night to these: so that the one came not near the other all the night. And Moses stretched out his hand over the sea; and the LORD caused the sea to go back by a strong east wind all that night, and made the sea dry land, and the waters were divided. And the children of Israel went into the midst of the sea upon the dry ground: and the waters were a wall unto them on their right hand, and on their left.—Exodus 14:19-22

While you watch with Jesus, His Spirit inspirits your spirit, enabling your spirit to separate from the flesh. When the separation is complete, the heavens part and you see Jesus. Conscious in His Spirit, you crossover.

> The Egyptians pursued, and went in after them to the midst of the sea, even all Pharaoh's horses, his chariots, and his horsemen. And it came to pass, that in the morning watch the LORD looked unto the host of the Egyptians through the pillar of fire and of the cloud, and troubled the host of the Egyptians, and took off their chariot wheels, that they drave them heavily: so that the Egyptians said, Let us flee from the face of Israel; for the LORD fighteth for them against the Egyptians.
> —Exodus 14:23-25

The Red Sea is the life and consciousness of mankind, a sea of blood wherein the flesh man dies, but the spirit man passes through and lives. When the children of Israel crossed the Red Sea, they crossed from flesh to spirit. They were, themselves, pillars of cloud and fire.

> The children of Israel walked upon dry land in the midst of the sea; and the waters were a wall unto them on their right hand, and on their left. Thus the LORD saved Israel that day out of the hand of the Egyptians; and Israel saw the Egyptians dead upon the sea shore. And Israel saw that great work which the LORD did upon the Egyptians: and the people feared the LORD, and believed the LORD, and his servant Moses.
> —Exodus 14:29-31

They saw "eye to eye" as the Spirit breathed within.[a]

---

[a] And when he had said this, he breathed on them, and saith unto them, "Receive ye the Holy Ghost."—John 20:22

THE EYE SINGLE

And they have said it unto the inhabitant of this land, they have heard that Thou, Jehovah, art in the midst of this people, that eye to eye Thou art seen—O Jehovah, and Thy cloud is standing over them,—and in a pillar of cloud Thou art going before them by day, and in a pillar of fire by night.
—Numbers 14:14 YLT

Bread From Heaven

AFTER more than a month of trekking through the wilderness, the Israelites hungered for the "flesh pots" of Egypt.

> And the whole congregation of the children of Israel murmured against Moses and Aaron in the wilderness: And the children of Israel said unto them, Would to God we had died by the hand of the LORD in the land of Egypt, when we sat by the flesh pots, and when we did eat bread to the full; for ye have brought us forth into this wilderness, to kill this whole assembly with hunger. —Exodus 16:2-3

The Eye Single

Without knowing it, the children of Israel spoke spiritual truth: flesh men waste in the wilderness, spirit men thrive.

> For if ye live after the flesh, ye shall die: but if ye through the Spirit do mortify the deeds of the body, ye shall live. —Romans 8:13

Moses and Aaron answered the children of Israel:

> At even, then ye shall know that the LORD hath brought you out from the land of Egypt: And in the morning, then ye shall see the glory of the LORD. —Exodus 16:6-7

First came flesh from heaven. Then came bread from heaven.

> It came to pass, that at even the quails came up, and covered the camp: and in the morning the dew lay round about the host. And when the dew that lay was gone up, behold, upon the face of the wilderness there lay a small round thing, as small as the hoar frost on the ground. And when the children of Israel saw it, they said one to another, It is manna: for they wist not what it was. And Moses said unto them, This is the bread which the LORD hath given you to eat. —Exodus 16:13-15

Jesus said:

> I am the living bread which came down from heaven: if any man eat of this bread, he shall live for ever: and the bread that I will give is my flesh, which I will give for the life of the world. —John 6:51

Jesus sacrificed His flesh that we might "see the glory of the LORD." *Seeing* the glory of the Lord is bread for the spirit.

> But we all, with open face beholding as in a glass the glory of the Lord, are changed into the same image from glory to glory, even as by the Spirit of the Lord.—2 Corinthians 3:18

Watch to see the Lord of glory.[1]

Gathering Manna

> Then said the LORD unto Moses, Behold, I will rain bread from heaven for you; and the people shall go out and gather a certain rate every day, that I may prove them, whether they will walk in my law, or no.—Exodus 16:4

The people had to humble themselves to get their day's portion of bread from heaven. Day after day, they rose to look for it; day after day, they knelt to gather it. Daily watching proves obedience, counts us worthy of the kingdom of God.

> And they gathered it every morning, every man according to his eating: and when the sun waxed hot, it melted.—Exodus 16:21

Manna fell with the dew, and like the dew it left with the sun. Watching is best done in the night watches.

> And Moses said, Let no man leave of it till the morning. Notwithstanding they hearkened not unto Moses; but some of them left of it until the morning, and it bred worms, and stank: and Moses was wroth with them.—Exodus 16:19-20

The Eye Single

What you gather, you must consume. If you choose sleep after gathering your omer of manna, if you "leave of it till the morning," expect negative, enervating effects. The manna will breed worms and stink. The bread from heaven must be assimilated in the light of consciousness ("when the sun waxed hot it melted"), not wasted and vitiated through sleep. Only on the eve of the Sabbath could they "leave of it till the morning," only on the sixth day could the Israelites gather a double portion.

> On the sixth day they gathered twice as much bread, two omers for one man: and all the rulers of the congregation came and told Moses. And he said unto them, This is that which the LORD hath said, To morrow is the rest of the holy sabbath unto the LORD: bake that which ye will bake to day, and seethe that ye will seethe; and that which remaineth over lay up for you to be kept until the morning. And they laid it up till the morning, as Moses bade: and it did not stink, neither was there any worm therein. And Moses said, Eat that to day; for to day is a sabbath unto the LORD: to day ye shall not find it in the field. Six days ye shall gather it; but on the seventh day, which is the sabbath, in it there shall be none. And it came to pass, that there went out some of the people on the seventh day for to gather, and they found none. And the LORD said unto Moses, How long refuse ye to keep my commandments and my laws? See, for that the LORD hath given you the sabbath, therefore he giveth you on the sixth day the bread of two days; abide ye every man in his place, let no man go out of his place on the seventh day. So the people rested on the seventh day. And the house of Israel called the

> name thereof Manna: and it was like coriander seed, white; and the taste of it was like wafers made with honey. — Exodus 16:22-31

The seventh day is the Sabbath — God's rest. His rest is our rest. Enter God's rest.

> There remaineth therefore a rest to the people of God. For he that is entered into his rest, he also hath ceased from his own works, as God did from his. — Hebrews 4:9-10

If you are diligent to gather your daily bread — watching every day — your appetite for manna will increase along with your capacity. When you are able to watch night and day, you will gather the double portion.[2] The double portion is life in the flesh plus life in the Spirit. Life in the Spirit of Jesus requires a second vessel, a spiritual body. Then every man will abide "in his place," every one will abide in God.

> Moses said, This is the thing which the LORD commandeth, Fill an omer of it to be kept for your generations; that they may see the bread wherewith I have fed you in the wilderness, when I brought you forth from the land of Egypt. And Moses said unto Aaron, Take a pot, and put an omer full of manna therein, and lay it up before the LORD, to be kept for your generations. As the LORD commanded Moses, so Aaron laid it up before the Testimony, to be kept. And the children of Israel did eat manna forty years, until they came to a land inhabited; they did eat manna, until they came unto the borders of the land of Canaan. — Exodus 16:32-35

The Eye Single

Hidden Manna

Jesus said, "*He that hath seen me hath seen the Father.*"³

> It came to pass, as he sat at meat with them, he took bread, and blessed it, and brake, and gave to them. And their eyes were opened, and they knew him; and he vanished out of their sight.
> —Luke 24:30-31

Watch with Jesus, ingest Jesus, until you see Jesus.

> Set your affection on things above, not on things on the earth. For ye are dead, and your life is hid with Christ in God. When Christ, who is our life, shall appear, then shall ye also appear with him in glory. —Colossians 3:2-4

Jesus is living bread, He is "the hidden manna."

> He that hath an ear, let him hear what the Spirit saith unto the churches; To him that overcometh will I give to eat of the hidden manna, and will give him a white stone, and in the stone a new name written, which no man knoweth saving he that receiveth it.
> —Revelation 2:17

"*What is it?*"[a]

What is the essence of watching? It is the mysterious impartation

---

[a] And when the children of Israel saw it, they said one to another, What is it? For they knew not what it was. And Moses said unto them, It is the bread which Jehovah hath given you to eat.—Exodus 16:15 ASV

of the life of Jesus, given that He might "do thee good" at your "latter end."

> Who fed thee in the wilderness with manna, which thy fathers knew not, that he might humble thee, and that he might prove thee, to do thee good at thy latter end. —Deuteronomy 8:16

Ask Me, Command Me

> Thus saith the LORD, the Holy One of Israel, and his Maker, Ask me of things to come concerning my sons, and concerning the work of my hands command ye me. —Isaiah 45:11

Jesus told a parable illustrating the manner of mind required of those who seek after God. The story involves three friends linked to one another by three loaves of bread.[b]

> Which of you shall have a friend, and shall go unto him at midnight, and say unto him, Friend, lend me three loaves; For a friend of mine in his journey is come to me, and I have nothing to set before him? And he from within shall answer and say, Trouble me not: the door is now shut, and my children are with me in bed; I cannot rise and give thee. I say unto you, Though he will not rise and give him, because he is his friend, yet because of his importunity he will rise and give him as many as he needeth. —Luke 11:5-8

---

[b] For there are three that bear record in heaven, the Father, the Word, and the Holy Ghost: and these three are one.—1 John 5:7

The Eye Single

Jesus is the friend who has arrived, and you are the friend with whom He is staying. You need bread from heaven to put before Him, spiritual sustenance for His spiritual body.

Our Father in heaven is the friend who has the bread of life, but He is in bed with His children. We have to wake Him. We have to go to Him at midnight and wake Him up. But first, we must wake ourselves, for God within must necessarily sleep as long as His children sleep: "Awake thou that sleepest, and arise from the dead, and Christ shall give thee light."[4]

Jesus tells us to be importunate in seeking the bread from heaven, and we will be importunate when we value the bread from heaven above everything else.

Then we will knock and keep on knocking, seek and keep on seeking, ask and keep on asking for the Holy Spirit.

> I say unto you, Ask, and it shall be given you; seek, and ye shall find; knock, and it shall be opened unto you. For every one that asketh receiveth; and he that seeketh findeth; and to him that knocketh it shall be opened. If a son shall ask bread of any of you that is a father, will he give him a stone? or if he ask a fish, will he for a fish give him a serpent? Or if he shall ask an egg, will he offer him a scorpion? If ye then, being evil, know how to give good gifts unto your children: how much more shall your heavenly Father give the Holy Spirit to them that ask him? — Luke 11:9-13

Our Father gives us everything when He gives us the Holy Spirit.

> But seek ye first the kingdom of God, and his righteousness; and all these things shall be added unto you. — Matthew 6:33

M̲ount S̲inai

T̲he L̲ord said unto Moses, Lo, I come unto thee in a thick cloud, that the people may hear when I speak with thee, and believe thee for ever. — Exodus 19:9

Because no one can endure gazing upon the source of love, light, and power, the Lord veiled His fiery self in a thick cloud.

> The L̲ord said unto Moses, Go unto the people, and sanctify them to day and to morrow, and let them wash their clothes. — Exodus 19:10

We need to be sanctified to meet the Lord. We need robes of

righteousness,[a] and "holiness, without which no man shall see the Lord."[1]

> Be ready against the third day: for the third day the LORD will come down in the sight of all the people upon mount Sinai. And thou shalt set bounds unto the people round about, saying, Take heed to yourselves, that ye go not up into the mount, or touch the border of it: whosoever toucheth the mount shall be surely put to death.
> —Exodus 19:11-12

Jesus' return will be as God coming down on Mount Sinai, "in the sight of all the people." Like Moses, we will rise to meet Him.[2] The spirit man will live, the flesh man "shall be surely put to death."

> There shall not an hand touch it, but he shall surely be stoned, or shot through; whether it be beast or man, it shall not live: when the trumpet soundeth long, they shall come up to the mount.
> —Exodus 19:13

Trumpets

Like a trumpet blown, a watcher's body transforms energy: energies of the flesh become energies of the spirit. The body sounds! At first, only a quiet stirring in the stillness, but as watching progresses and the spirit is enlivened, the sound intensifies. When the spirit is about to separate from the flesh and

---

[a] These are they which came out of great tribulation, and have washed their robes, and made them white in the blood of the Lamb.—Revelation 7:14

ascend in consciousness, spiritual energy is both heard and felt. The body becomes a Jacob's ladder! Power pours into it.

You are a trumpet: a ram's horn (Jesus is the ram[b]) caught in the thicket of life,[c] a ram's horn to be filled with the oil of the Spirit.

> But my horn shalt thou exalt like the horn of an unicorn: I shall be anointed with fresh oil.
> —Psalms 92:10

A ram's horn sounding the Spirit's transforming power. Wait until "the trumpet soundeth long." Await "the last trump" that immediately precedes and accompanies the return of our Lord,[3] which signals the breakthrough into the Spirit of God.[d]

> Behold, I shew you a mystery; We shall not all sleep, but we shall all be changed, In a moment, in the twinkling of an eye, at the last trump: for the trumpet shall sound, and the dead shall be raised incorruptible, and we shall be changed. For this corruptible must put on incorruption, and this mortal must put on immortality. So when this corruptible shall have put on incorruption, and this mortal shall have

---

[b] And I beheld, and, lo, in the midst of the throne and of the four beasts, and in the midst of the elders, stood a Lamb as it had been slain, having seven horns and seven eyes, which are the seven Spirits of God sent forth into all the earth. —Revelation 5:6

[c] And Abraham lifted up his eyes, and looked, and behold behind him a ram caught in a thicket by his horns: and Abraham went and took the ram, and offered him up for a burnt offering in the stead of his son.—Genesis 22:13

[d] When they make a long blast with the ram's horn, and when ye hear the sound of the trumpet, all the people shall shout with a great shout; and the wall of the city shall fall down flat, and the people shall ascend up every man straight before him.—Joshua 6:5

put on immortality, then shall be brought to pass the saying that is written, Death is swallowed up in victory. —1 Corinthians 15:51-54

Fire And Smoke

Moses brought forth the people out of the camp to meet with God; and they stood at the nether part of the mount. And mount Sinai was altogether on a smoke, because the LORD descended upon it in fire: and the smoke thereof ascended as the smoke of a furnace, and the whole mount quaked greatly.
—Exodus 19:17-18

To leave the camp to meet with God is to leave all for Jesus.

Every one that hath forsaken houses, or brethren, or sisters, or father, or mother, or wife, or children, or lands, for my name's sake, shall receive an hundredfold, and shall inherit everlasting life.
—Matthew 19:29

The people watched and waited at the foot of the mountain. It was their watching and waiting that brought down the Consuming Fire.

Seeing then that all these things shall be dissolved, what manner of persons ought ye to be in all holy conversation and godliness, Looking for and hasting unto the coming of the day of God, wherein the heavens being on fire shall be dissolved, and the elements shall melt with fervent heat? —2 Peter 3:11-12

"The whole mount quaked greatly."

> Now when the centurion, and they that were with him, watching Jesus, saw the earthquake, and those things that were done, they feared greatly, saying, Truly this was the Son of God.
> —Matthew 27:54

Thunder And Lightning

> It came to pass on the third day in the morning, that there were thunders and lightnings, and a thick cloud upon the mount, and the voice of the trumpet exceeding loud; so that all the people that was in the camp trembled.
> —Exodus 19:16

When God is about to reveal Himself from within the thick cloud of spirit, there are effects in consciousness akin to thunder and lightning and the voice of an "exceeding loud" trumpet. The spirit, mind, and body tremble with power. It is a sign to watch continually. You will hear and feel a whirlwind of power before the spirit man ascends in consciousness and you receive your double portion. Like Stephen, you will glow with angelic light.[4] Like John, you will hear a great voice as "a trumpet talking" saying, *"Come up hither!"*

> After this I looked, and, behold, a door was opened in heaven: and the first voice which I heard was as it were of a trumpet talking with me; which said, Come up hither, and I will shew thee things which must be hereafter.
> —Revelation 4:1

The Eye Single

Like lightning, the power of God will cause the heavens to open.

> And immediately I was in the spirit: and, behold, a throne was set in heaven, and one sat on the throne. And he that sat was to look upon like a jasper and a sardine stone: and there was a rainbow round about the throne, in sight like unto an emerald. —Revelation 4:2-3

Dialogue

"When the voice of the trumpet sounded long, and waxed louder and louder, Moses spake, and God answered him by a voice."[5] What did Moses speak? Scripture is silent. He spoke … a word.[e] Jesus is the Word spoken.[f] He who is one with the Word speaks the Word![g]

> What I tell you in darkness, that speak ye in light: and what ye hear in the ear, that preach ye upon the housetops. —Matthew 10:27

To hear the Word spoken from the midst of Fire is a wondrous and glorious thing. But to hear is to die.

> Behold, the LORD our God hath shewed us his glory and his greatness, and we have heard his voice out of the midst of the fire: we have seen this day that God doth talk with man, and he

---

[e] In the beginning was the Word, and the Word was with God, and the Word was God.—John 1:1

[f] And the Word was made flesh, and dwelt among us, (and we beheld his glory, the glory as of the only begotten of the Father,) full of grace and truth.—John 1:14

[g] If ye abide in me, and my words abide in you, ye shall ask what ye will, and it shall be done unto you.—John 15:7

FROM DARKNESS TO LIGHT • Mount Sinai

> liveth. Now therefore why should we die? For this great fire will consume us: if we hear the voice of the LORD our God any more, then we shall die. For who is there of all flesh, that hath heard the voice of the living God speaking out of the midst of the fire, as we have, and lived?
> —Deuteronomy 5:24-26

Life in Jesus costs life in the flesh.

> He that findeth his life shall lose it: and he that loseth his life for my sake shall find it.
> —Matthew 10:39

When His anointing is upon you, look for Him. When He calls you, go to Him.[h] Like a monarch from its chrysalis, ascend!

> And the LORD came down upon mount Sinai, on the top of the mount: and the LORD called Moses up to the top of the mount; and Moses went up. —Exodus 19:20

Calling Down The Man of God

> The LORD said unto Moses, Go down, charge the people, lest they break through unto the LORD to gaze, and many of them perish. And let the priests also, which come near to the LORD, sanctify themselves, lest the LORD break forth upon them. —Exodus 19:21-22

Watching is a boundary experience: you are where God meets

---

[h] My sheep hear my voice, and I know them, and they follow me.—John 10:27

man; you are in His presence. Only those who love Jesus and long for His appearing should watch.[i] There is danger in calling down the Man of God. The power of His presence cuts like a double-edged sword—for and against. The spirit lives, the flesh dies.

> The king [Ahaziah] sent unto him a captain of fifty with his fifty. And he went up to him: and, behold, he sat on the top of an hill. And he spake unto him, Thou man of God, the king hath said, Come down. And Elijah answered and said to the captain of fifty, If I be a man of God, then let fire come down from heaven, and consume thee and thy fifty. And there came down fire from heaven, and consumed him and his fifty. Again also he sent unto him another captain of fifty with his fifty. And he answered and said unto him, O man of God, thus hath the king said, Come down quickly. And Elijah answered and said unto them, If I be a man of God, let fire come down from heaven, and consume thee and thy fifty. And the fire of God came down from heaven, and consumed him and his fifty.—2 Kings 1:9-12

The Man of God esteems those who fear Him enough to humble themselves; their lives are precious in His sight.

> And he sent again a captain of the third fifty with his fifty. And the third captain of fifty went up, and came and fell on his knees before Elijah, and besought him, and said unto him,

---
[i] He that believeth on the Son hath everlasting life: and he that believeth not the Son shall not see life; but the wrath of God abideth on him.—John 3:36

> O man of God, I pray thee, let my life, and the life of these fifty thy servants, be precious in thy sight. Behold, there came fire down from heaven, and burnt up the two captains of the former fifties with their fifties: therefore let my life now be precious in thy sight. And the angel of the LORD said unto Elijah, Go down with him: be not afraid of him. And he arose, and went down with him unto the king.
> —2 Kings 1:13-15

Daily watching builds power for a spiritual breakthrough that we experience as God's break forth.[j] Let us, who "love His appearing,"[6] pray with the prophet:

> Oh that thou wouldest rend the heavens, that thou wouldest come down, that the mountains might flow down at thy presence, As when the melting fire burneth, the fire causeth the waters to boil, to make thy name known to thine adversaries, that the nations may tremble at thy presence! When thou didst terrible things which we looked not for, thou camest down, the mountains flowed down at thy presence. For since the beginning of the world men have not heard, nor perceived by the ear, neither hath the eye seen, O God, beside thee, what he hath prepared for him that waiteth for him.—Isaiah 64:1-4

---

[j] Jesus' breakthrough to life in the Spirit came after John baptized Him: "And straightway coming up out of the water, he saw the heavens opened, and the Spirit like a dove descending upon him."—Mark 1:10

The Eye Single

The Third Day

> And he said unto the people, Be ready against the third day: come not at your wives.
> —Exodus 19:15

This world is beautiful, its pleasures desirable, and it is "very good,"[k] but do not be possessed by it.[l] Seek the greater beauty and greater pleasure of the world to come.

> Eye hath not seen, nor ear heard, neither have entered into the heart of man, the things which God hath prepared for them that love him.
> —1 Corinthians 2:9

To make the breakthrough into the Spirit of God, your life force must be wholly focused on Jesus' return. "Be ready against the third day."

> The time is short: it remaineth, that both they that have wives be as though they had none; and they that weep, as though they wept not; and they that rejoice, as though they rejoiced not; and they that buy, as though they possessed not; and they that use this world, as not abusing it: for the fashion of this world passeth away.
> —1 Corinthians 7:29-31

Lay down your life to take it up again. Lose it to find it.

---

[k] And God saw every thing that he had made, and, behold, it was very good. —Genesis 1:31

[l] All things are lawful unto me, but all things are not expedient: all things are lawful for me, but I will not be brought under the power of any. —1 Corinthians 6:12

> For whosoever will save his life shall lose it: and whosoever will lose his life for my sake shall find it.—Matthew 16:25

For a season, forgo what is good for what is transcendent.[m] "The time is short." Wait, and He will come.

> My soul waiteth in silence for God only: From him cometh my salvation.—Psalms 62:1 ASV

---

[m] Defraud ye not one the other, except it be with consent for a time, that ye may give yourselves to fasting and prayer; and come together again, that Satan tempt you not for your incontinency.—1 Corinthians 7:5

Built By God

I HEARD a great voice out of heaven saying, Behold, the tabernacle of God is with men, and he will dwell with them, and they shall be his people, and God himself shall be with them, and be their God.
—Revelation 21:3

After leaving Egypt, the first encampment of the Israelites was at Succoth. The name, which means *booths* or *tabernacles*,[1] signified the temporary dwellings that the Israelites lived in during their forty years of wanderings in the wilderness. God instituted the Feast of Tabernacles as a remembrance:

> Ye shall dwell in booths seven days; all that are Israelites born shall dwell in booths: That your generations may know that I made the children of Israel to dwell in booths, when I brought them out of the land of Egypt. —Leviticus 23:42-43

Similarly, Christians live in booths on their journey to Jesus. Your booth is your spiritual body (an eternal tabernacle), which is forming within after His likeness, for whom:

> He did foreknow, he also did predestinate to be conformed to the image of his Son, that he might be the firstborn among many brethren.
> —Romans 8:29

Your physical body is also a tabernacle, a temporary tabernacle.

> I think it meet, as long as I am in this tabernacle, to stir you up by putting you in remembrance; Knowing that shortly I must put off this my tabernacle, even as our Lord Jesus Christ hath shewed me. —2 Peter 1:13-14

When you put off your temporal tabernacle, you put on your eternal tabernacle. For we "know that if our earthly house of this tabernacle were dissolved, we have a building of God, an house not made with hands, eternal in the heavens." [2] The eternal tabernacle is not of this world. It is "afar off from the camp." [3]

> Wherefore Jesus also, that he might sanctify the people with his own blood, suffered without the gate. Let us go forth therefore unto him without the camp, bearing his reproach. For here have we no continuing city, but we seek one to come.
> —Hebrews 13:12-14

The Eye Single

Your physical body houses your soul until death; the spiritual body houses it for eternity.

> For which cause we faint not; but though our outward man perish, yet the inward man is renewed day by day. —2 Corinthians 4:16

A watcher lives in the spiritual body while alive in the physical body. You die before you die; you die to the world.

> For ye are dead, and your life is hid with Christ in God. —Colossians 3:3

A House Of Watching

> It came to pass, when Moses went out unto the tabernacle, that all the people rose up, and stood every man at his tent door, and looked after Moses, until he was gone into the tabernacle. And it came to pass, as Moses entered into the tabernacle, the cloudy pillar descended, and stood at the door of the tabernacle, and the LORD talked with Moses. And all the people saw the cloudy pillar stand at the tabernacle door: and all the people rose up and worshipped, every man in his tent door.
> —Exodus 33:8-10

Moses is a figure of the Christian whose soul seeks union with Jesus in the tabernacle of spirit. When you rise up to watch at the door of your physical tabernacle, your soul enters the spiritual tabernacle. As you continue to watch, the Lord descends to the door of the tabernacle to commune with you. The door to the tabernacle of spirit is the eye.

> The light of the body is the eye: if therefore
> thine eye be single, thy whole body shall be full
> of light. —Matthew 6:22

Moses' face shone from being in the presence of the Lord.[4]

> And when Aaron and all the children of Israel
> saw Moses, behold, the skin of his face shone;
> and they were afraid to come nigh him.
> —Exodus 34:30

Moses saw Jesus, "the image of the invisible God."[5] He spoke with Jesus, the shape and similitude of God.

> And the LORD spake unto Moses face to face,
> as a man speaketh unto his friend.
> —Exodus 33:11

Moses spoke "face to face." He had the same face, the same mind, the same heart. Not only was Moses a friend of God, he was one with God. He glowed God's glory.

> And the glory which thou gavest me I have
> given them; that they may be one, even as we
> are one. —John 17:22

When Moses left the Tabernacle, his servant, Joshua, "departed not out of the tabernacle."[6] It was Joshua who made Moses' union with God possible. Joshua is Jesus.[7]

> For Christ is not entered into the holy places made
> with hands, which are the figures of the true; but
> into heaven itself, now to appear in the presence
> of God for us. —Hebrews 9:24

THE EYE SINGLE

To watch with Jesus is to behold the glory of the Lord.

> For God, who commanded the light to shine out of darkness, hath shined in our hearts, to give the light of the knowledge of the glory of God in the face of Jesus Christ. —2 Corinthians 4:6

Beholding the glory of the Lord, we "put on the new man, which after God is created in righteousness and true holiness."[8] We form new tabernacles that are ever-greater approximations of the body of knowledge we will receive when we see Jesus.

> But put ye on the Lord Jesus Christ, and make not provision for the flesh, to fulfil the lusts thereof.
> —Romans 13:14

We shall see Jesus as He is after we have gone "from glory to glory," after we have been changed into His image. We will see Him when we are like Him.

The Tabernacle And Cherubim

GOD told Moses, "Let them make me a sanctuary; that I may dwell among them."[1] The sanctuary was called the Tabernacle of the Congregation,[2] a model of the Christian sanctuary.

> For ye are the temple of the living God; as God hath said, I will dwell in them, and walk in them; and I will be their God, and they shall be my people. —2 Corinthians 6:16

The Tabernacle had curtains for walls and a veil that separated the Holy Place from the Most Holy. The curtains and veil were embroidered with images of extraordinary living creatures called cherubim.[3] Within the Most Holy Place, two golden cherubim with wings extended stood opposite each other on top of the ark, their faces turned toward the mercy seat.

> He made two cherubims of gold, beaten out of one piece made he them, on the two ends of the mercy seat; One cherub on the end on this side, and another cherub on the other end on that side: out of the mercy seat made he the cherubims on the two ends thereof. And the cherubims spread out their wings on high, and covered with their wings over the mercy seat, with their faces one to another; even to the mercy seatward were the faces of the cherubims.
> —Exodus 37:7-9

The mercy seat that the cherubim gazed upon is Jesus:

> Whom God did set forth a mercy seat, through the faith in his blood. —Romans 3:25 YLT

Like the cherubim, Christians fix their gaze upon Jesus. We *see* Him. We are "of one piece." He is the vine; we are the branches.[4] He is our life; we are His body.

> Now ye are the body of Christ, and members in particular. —1 Corinthians 12:27

On the Day of Atonement, the high priest sprinkled the blood of the sin offering upon the mercy seat:

> Then shall he kill the goat of the sin offering, that is for the people, and bring his blood within the vail, and do with that blood as he did with the blood of the bullock, and sprinkle it upon

> the mercy seat, and before the mercy seat: And he shall make an atonement for the holy place, because of the uncleanness of the children of Israel, and because of their transgressions in all their sins: and so shall he do for the tabernacle of the congregation, that remaineth among them in the midst of their uncleanness.
> —Leviticus 16:15-16

Jesus is our high priest.

> But Christ being come an high priest of good things to come, by a greater and more perfect tabernacle, not made with hands, that is to say, not of this building; Neither by the blood of goats and calves, but by his own blood he entered in once into the holy place, having obtained eternal redemption for us.
> —Hebrews 9:11-12

He is the sin offering. He is our lifeblood.

> Then Jesus said unto them, Verily, verily, I say unto you, Except ye eat the flesh of the Son of man, and drink his blood, ye have no life in you.—John 6:53

Meet Him above the mercy seat, between "the cherubims of glory."[a] Meet in the midst of watching eyes.

> There I will meet with thee, and I will commune

---

[a] And over it the cherubims of glory shadowing the mercy seat; of which we cannot now speak particularly.—Hebrews 9:5

The Eye Single

> with thee from above the mercy seat, from between the two cherubims which are upon the ark of the testimony, of all things which I will give thee in commandment unto the children of Israel.
> —Exodus 25:22

The Cherubim Of The Heavenly Temple

God gave Ezekiel a vision of a future temple. The doors leading into the sanctuary, and all the interior walls, were decorated with carvings of cherubim with two faces—that of a man and a lion.[5] Each face gazed upon a palm tree:

> It was made with cherubims and palm trees, so that a palm tree was between a cherub and a cherub; and every cherub had two faces; So that the face of a man was toward the palm tree on the one side, and the face of a young lion toward the palm tree on the other side: it was made through all the house round about. From the ground unto above the door were cherubims and palm trees made, and on the wall of the temple.
> —Ezekiel 41:18-20

To desert people, palm trees are trees of life.[b] Watchers are desert people; we watch with Jesus—the Lion of Judah—our tree of life.[6]

> To him that overcometh will I give to eat of the tree of life, which is in the midst of the paradise of God. —Revelation 2:7

To see Him, we pass through the enfolding fire.

---

[b] Wherever palm trees are there is an oasis of dates, water, and shade.

> So he drove out the man; and he placed at the east of the garden of Eden Cherubims, and a flaming sword which turned every way, to keep the way of the tree of life. — Genesis 3:24

The Cherubim Chariot Of God

Ezekiel had a vision in which the heavens were opened. He "saw visions of God."[7] He saw the chariot of God! He saw "living creatures," which were four cherubim, all with the likeness of a man, but with four faces and four wings. A wheel was beside each cherub, and they were "full of eyes round about, even the wheels that they four had." Above the cherubim was a firmament, above the firmament a throne, and upon the throne was God in the likeness of a glorious man.

> I looked, and, behold, a whirlwind came out of the north, a great cloud, and a fire infolding itself, and a brightness was about it, and out of the midst thereof as the colour of amber, out of the midst of the fire. Also out of the midst thereof came the likeness of four living creatures. And this was their appearance; they had the likeness of a man. And every one had four faces, and every one had four wings. And their feet were straight feet; and the sole of their feet was like the sole of a calf's foot: and they sparkled like the colour of burnished brass. And they had the hands of a man under their wings on their four sides; and they four had their faces and their wings. Their wings were joined one to another; they turned not when they went; they went every one straight forward. As for the likeness of their faces, they four had the face of a

> man, and the face of a lion, on the right side: and they four had the face of an ox on the left side; they four also had the face of an eagle.
> —Ezekiel 1:4-10

The spirit of the living creatures was in the wheels that whirled beside them.[8]

> And I looked, and behold, four wheels beside the cherubim, one wheel beside one cherub, and another wheel beside another cherub; and the appearance of the wheels was like unto a beryl stone. And as for their appearance, they four had one likeness, as if a wheel had been within a wheel. When they went, they went in their four directions: they turned not as they went, but to the place whither the head looked they followed it; they turned not as they went. And their whole body, and their backs, and their hands, and their wings, and the wheels, were full of eyes round about, even the wheels that they four had. As for the wheels, they were called in my hearing, the whirling wheels.—Ezekiel 10:9-13 ASV

The power of the Spirit, as evidenced in watching, is illustrated by the wheels "full of eyes" that moved "to the place whither the head looked." The eye that focuses upon Jesus forms a wheel of consciousness in both the spirit and the flesh, "as if a wheel had been in the midst of a wheel." Like whirlwinds, these "whirling wheels" of spiritual consciousness draw energy and power into the life of the watcher.

> When the cherubim went, the wheels went beside them; and when the cherubim lifted up their wings

> to mount up from the earth, the wheels also turned not from beside them. When they stood, these stood; and when they mounted up, these mounted up with them: for the spirit of the living creature was in them. —Ezekiel 10:16-17 ASV

Watchers *see* God until they see God.

> Over the head of the living creature there was the likeness of a firmament, like the terrible crystal to look upon, stretched forth over their heads above.
> —Ezekiel 1:22 ASV

Spiritual consciousness is the firmament upon which God appears.

> Above the firmament that was over their heads was the likeness of a throne, as the appearance of a sapphire stone: and upon the likeness of the throne was the likeness as the appearance of a man above upon it. And I saw as the colour of amber, as the appearance of fire round about within it, from the appearance of his loins even upward, and from the appearance of his loins even downward, I saw as it were the appearance of fire, and it had brightness round about. As the appearance of the bow that is in the cloud in the day of rain, so was the appearance of round about. This was the appearance of the likeness of the glory of the LORD. And when I saw it, I fell upon my face, and I heard a voice of one that spake. And he said unto me, Son of man, stand upon thy feet, and I will speak unto thee.
> —Ezekiel 1:26-2:1

The Eye Single

Why do the cherubim—these amazing "living creatures"—have such prominence in the presence of God? Do they image the Christian (man) in whom Jesus (the Lion of Judah) lives? When Jesus enters your heart, He tames your animal nature by cutting away the flesh (the ox),[c] making you alive in the Spirit (the eagle).

> And he rode upon a cherub, and did fly: and he was seen upon the wings of the wind.
> —2 Samuel 22:11

---

[c] And ye are complete in him, which is the head of all principality and power: In whom also ye are circumcised with the circumcision made without hands, in putting off the body of the sins of the flesh by the circumcision of Christ. —Colossians 2:10-11

I Am

> GOD said unto Moses, I AM THAT I AM: and he said, Thus shalt thou say unto the children of Israel, I AM hath sent me unto you. And God said moreover unto Moses, Thus shalt thou say unto the children of Israel, The LORD God of your fathers, the God of Abraham, the God of Isaac, and the God of Jacob, hath sent me unto you: this is my name for ever, and this is my memorial unto all generations. — Exodus 3:14-15

God's quintessential name is "I AM," a name that is at once no name and every name. No name can encompass Him. He is a phenomenon. He is an experience.

The Eye Single

> I am Alpha and Omega, the beginning and the ending, saith the Lord, which is, and which was, and which is to come, the Almighty.
> —Revelation 1:8

We can only comment on His attributes: love and light, justice and mercy, vengeance and wrath.

> I am the LORD, and there is none else. I form the light, and create darkness: I make peace, and create evil: I the LORD do all these things.
> —Isaiah 45:6-7

The Lord God, I AM, "in whose hand is the soul of every living thing, and the breath of all mankind,"[1] is known instantly by the believer. He calls your name.

Say, *"Here am I. Look at me, see me."*

He is always present; be present with Him.

> Jesus said, I am: and ye shall see the Son of man sitting on the right hand of power, and coming in the clouds of heaven. —Mark 14:62

Here Am I

A shepherd shepherds his life when he shepherds his sheep. Moses brought his sheep ever deeper into the desert until he arrived at the mountain of God and met God in the burning bush.

> Now Moses kept the flock of Jethro his father in law, the priest of Midian: and he led the flock to the backside of the desert, and came to the mountain of God, even to Horeb. And the angel of the LORD appeared unto him in a flame of fire out of the midst of a bush: and he looked, and,

> behold, the bush burned with fire, and the bush was not consumed. And Moses said, I will now turn aside, and see this great sight, why the bush is not burnt. And when the LORD saw that he turned aside to see, God called unto him out of the midst of the bush, and said, Moses, Moses. And he said, Here am I. And he said, Draw not nigh hither: put off thy shoes from off thy feet, for the place whereon thou standest is holy ground.
> —Exodus 3:1-5

When Moses turned aside to "see this great sight," God called his name, "*Moses, Moses.*"

Moses responded, "*Here am I.*"

Moses was present with God; he saw the One who sees within.

> Sing and rejoice, O daughter of Zion: for, lo, I come, and I will dwell in the midst of thee.
> —Zechariah 2:10

Moses, himself, was the bush that God burned within.[a] His soul's many traits were the bush's many branches.

> And they said one to another, Did not our heart burn within us, while he talked with us by the way, and while he opened to us the scriptures?
> —Luke 24:32

Reasoning With I AM

Moses, the meekest of men,[b] found grace in the sight of the watcher of men. God's sight is God's consciousness. God knew

---

[a] I am the vine, ye are the branches.—John 15:5

[b] (Now the man Moses was very meek, above all the men which were upon the face of the earth.)—Numbers 12:3

The Eye Single

Moses because Moses lived in His consciousness; he was a friend of God with the mind of God.

> The LORD said unto Moses, Go, get thee down; for thy people, which thou broughtest out of the land of Egypt, have corrupted themselves: They have turned aside quickly out of the way which I commanded them: they have made them a molten calf, and have worshipped it, and have sacrificed thereunto, and said, These be thy gods, O Israel, which have brought thee up out of the land of Egypt. And the LORD said unto Moses, I have seen this people, and, behold, it is a stiffnecked people: Now therefore let me alone, that my wrath may wax hot against them, and that I may consume them: and I will make of thee a great nation. — Exodus 32:7-10

Why would God say to Moses, "*let me alone*"? What power over God did Moses have? Moses had the power of relationship: he loved God and knew Him by name. He also knew God had promised the land of Canaan to the descendants of Abraham, Isaac, and Israel:

> Moses besought the LORD his God, and said, LORD, why doth thy wrath wax hot against thy people, which thou hast brought forth out of the land of Egypt with great power, and with a mighty hand? Wherefore should the Egyptians speak, and say, For mischief did he bring them out, to slay them in the mountains, and to consume them from the face of the earth? Turn from thy fierce wrath, and repent of this evil against thy people. Remember Abraham, Isaac,

> and Israel, thy servants, to whom thou swarest by thine own self, and saidst unto them, I will multiply your seed as the stars of heaven, and all this land that I have spoken of will I give unto your seed, and they shall inherit it for ever. And the LORD repented of the evil which he thought to do unto his people.
> —Exodus 32:11-14

Moses had put God "in remembrance,"[c] and God "repented of the evil which he thought to do." But He had not relented:

> Depart, and go up hence, thou and the people which thou hast brought up out of the land of Egypt, unto the land which I sware unto Abraham, to Isaac, and to Jacob, saying, Unto thy seed will I give it: And I will send an angel before thee; and I will drive out the Canaanite, the Amorite, and the Hittite, and the Perizzite, the Hivite, and the Jebusite: Unto a land flowing with milk and honey: for I will not go up in the midst of thee; for thou art a stiffnecked people: lest I consume thee in the way. —Exodus 33:1-3

Their situation was still dire, for who and what are the people of God without God?

> But ye are not in the flesh, but in the Spirit, if so be that the Spirit of God dwell in you. Now if any man have not the Spirit of Christ, he is none of his. —Romans 8:9

---

[c] Put me in remembrance: let us plead together: declare thou, that thou mayest be justified.—Isaiah 43:26

The Eye Single

Moses interceded again:

> If thy presence go not with me, carry us not up hence. For wherein shall it be known here that I and thy people have found grace in thy sight? is it not in that thou goest with us? so shall we be separated, I and thy people, from all the people that are upon the face of the earth. And the LORD said unto Moses, I will do this thing also that thou hast spoken: for thou hast found grace in my sight, and I know thee by name. —Exodus 33:15-17

Our heavenly Father, more than any earthly father, desires to live life with His children. He sent His son, Jesus. Through Jesus, He abides in us. He hears our prayers, He gives us rest.

> Come unto me, all ye that labour and are heavy laden, and I will give you rest. Take my yoke upon you, and learn of me; for I am meek and lowly in heart: and ye shall find rest unto your souls. For my yoke is easy, and my burden is light. —Matthew 11:28-30

God speaks with those who will listen, who obey.

> The LORD God will do nothing, but he revealeth his secret unto his servants the prophets.
> —Amos 3:7

He looks for men who will help Him establish His name upon the earth, men to instruct us to be as He is—righteous and holy, just and merciful.

> I sought for a man among them, that should

> make up the hedge, and stand in the gap before me for the land, that I should not destroy it: but I found none. —Ezekiel 22:30

Moses was one who stood in the gap before the Lord.[2] Because he had found grace in God's sight, his pleading became imaging in God's sight. His demand, command. His expressed desire, the Word spoken.

> Have faith of God. For truly I say to you, Whoever says to this mountain, Be taken up and be thrown into the sea, and does not doubt in his heart, but believes that what he says will happen, it will be to him, whatever he says.
> —Mark 11:22-23 LITV

Moses is the spiritually alive man who sees God face to face. God knows him by name and speaks to him in plain words.[3]

> With him will I speak mouth to mouth, even apparently, and not in dark speeches; and the similitude of the LORD shall he behold: wherefore then were ye not afraid to speak against my servant Moses? —Numbers 12:8

Like Moses, Christians will see "the similitude of the LORD." We will see and speak with Jesus.

> Ye now therefore have sorrow: but I will see you again, and your heart shall rejoice, and your joy no man taketh from you. And in that day ye shall ask me nothing. Verily, verily, I say unto you, Whatsoever ye shall ask the Father in my name, he will give it you. —John 16:22-23

The Eye Single

We look for Jesus, who is "the brightness of his glory, and the express image of his person."[4]

> This is the will of him that sent me, that every one which seeth the Son, and believeth on him, may have everlasting life: and I will raise him up at the last day. —John 6:40

God As Self

>   *T*HUS saith the LORD, Let not the wise man glory in his wisdom, neither let the mighty man glory in his might, let not the rich man glory in his riches: But let him that glorieth glory in this, that he understandeth and knoweth me, that I am the LORD which exercise lovingkindness, judgment, and righteousness, in the earth: for in these things I delight, saith the LORD.
> —Jeremiah 9:23-24

God wants relationship and He found it with Moses. Moses' prayers and supplications to the God 'out there' brought him to

The Eye Single

awareness and knowledge of the One who lives within. He conversed with our Father like we dialogue with ourselves, for God is both within and without. When Moses reasoned with God, he reasoned with God as self! Moses wanted God to look at things his way, and God did. As Moses believed, so it was done.[a]

Twice Moses spent forty days and forty nights alone with God on Mount Sinai. During that time he neither ate nor drank, the Lord sustained Him.[1] When he came down from the mount, his face shone, for the Spirit of God was within him. It shone as did another's on a different mount over a thousand years later:

> As he prayed, the fashion of his countenance was altered, and his raiment was white and glistering. And, behold, there talked with him two men, which were Moses and Elias: Who appeared in glory, and spake of his decease which he should accomplish at Jerusalem. —Luke 9:29-31

Moses entered into the presence of Love and Light to commune with the Spirit of truth. The spirit of Jesus is the Spirit of truth:

> I will pray the Father, and he shall give you another Comforter, that he may abide with you for ever; Even the Spirit of truth; whom the world cannot receive, because it seeth him not, neither knoweth him: but ye know him; for he dwelleth with you, and shall be in you.
> —John 14:16-17

Moses was a type of the Anointed One, the Messiah, the Prophet

---

[a] And Jesus said unto the centurion, Go thy way; and as thou hast believed, so be it done unto thee. And his servant was healed in the selfsame hour.
—Matthew 8:13; 1 John 3:22

who is Christ Jesus.[b] The Spirit of God was upon him to speak His words and work His works.[c] However, when the care of the people became too much for Moses, God "took of the spirit that was upon him" and placed it upon seventy elders of Israel to help bear the burden:[d]

> Moses went out, and told the people the words of the LORD, and gathered the seventy men of the elders of the people, and set them round about the tabernacle. And the LORD came down in a cloud, and spake unto him, and took of the spirit that was upon him, and gave it unto the seventy elders: and it came to pass, that, when the spirit rested upon them, they prophesied, and did not cease. But there remained two of the men in the camp, the name of the one was Eldad, and the name of the other Medad: and the spirit rested upon them; and they were of them that were written, but went not out unto the tabernacle: and they prophesied in the camp. And there ran a young man, and told Moses, and said, Eldad and Medad do prophesy in the camp. And Joshua the son of Nun, the servant of Moses, one of his young men, answered and said, My lord Moses, forbid them. And Moses said unto

---

[b] I will raise them up a Prophet from among their brethren, like unto thee, and will put my words in his mouth; and he shall speak unto them all that I shall command him.—Deuteronomy 18:18

[c] Now therefore go, and I will be with thy mouth, and teach thee what thou shalt say.—Exodus 4:12

[d] Now after these things the LORD appointed seventy others, and sent them two and two before his face into every city and place, whither he himself was about to come.—Luke 10:1 ASV; Numbers 11:17

The Eye Single

> him, Enviest thou for my sake? Would God that all the LORD'S people were prophets, and that the LORD would put his spirit upon them!
> —Numbers 11:24-29

If you have given yourself to Jesus, Jesus is your self. His Spirit is upon you as it was upon Moses. Like Moses, you are a face of the One who lives within you. You are a face of the Father through the Son. Jesus prayed:

> And now, O Father, glorify thou me with thine own self with the glory which I had with thee before the world was. —John 17:5

Then He prayed the same for us:

> Neither pray I for these alone, but for them also which shall believe on me through their word; That they all may be one; as thou, Father, art in me, and I in thee, that they also may be one in us: that the world may believe that thou hast sent me. And the glory which thou gavest me I have given them; that they may be one, even as we are one: I in them, and thou in me, that they may be made perfect in one; and that the world may know that thou hast sent me, and hast loved them, as thou hast loved me. Father, I will that they also, whom thou hast given me, be with me where I am; that they may behold my glory, which thou hast given me: for thou lovedst me before the foundation of the world.
> —John 17:20-24

The Father glorified Jesus, the Son of man, with His own self.

Then Jesus, the Son, glorified us with the same self that we might be one with the Father as He is one with the Father. God, your Father, lives in you as your own self!

> Examine yourselves, whether ye be in the faith; prove your own selves. Know ye not your own selves, how that Jesus Christ is in you, except ye be reprobates?—2 Corinthians 13:5

When Jesus ascended to the Father, He brought mankind with Him. He divinized humanity. He humanized God.

> Jesus saith unto her, Touch me not; for I am not yet ascended to my Father: but go to my brethren, and say unto them, I ascend unto my Father, and your Father; and to my God, and your God.—John 20:17

Jesus said we can move mountains if we believe what we say will come to pass. Yet it is God, and only God, who moves mountains—God in us. He is the Power of faith filled words.

> When the multitudes saw it [the healing of the paralytic], they marvelled, and glorified God, which had given such power unto men.
> —Matthew 9:8

As Moses reminded God that the Hebrews were His people, so Christians ought to remind themselves who they are in Jesus. We are sons and daughters of our Father God, who has sent His Spirit to live in us and bring us to the knowledge of His Son.

> For as many as are led by the Spirit of God, they are the sons of God.—Romans 8:14

The Eye Single

Christian, may you "be filled with all the fullness of God."

> For this cause I bow my knees unto the Father of our Lord Jesus Christ, Of whom the whole family in heaven and earth is named, That he would grant you, according to the riches of his glory, to be strengthened with might by his Spirit in the inner man; That Christ may dwell in your hearts by faith; that ye, being rooted and grounded in love, May be able to comprehend with all saints what is the breadth, and length, and depth, and height; And to know the love of Christ, which passeth knowledge, that ye might be filled with all the fulness of God.
> —Ephesians 3:14-19

Glory

> He said, I beseech thee, shew me thy glory. And he said, I will make all my goodness pass before thee, and I will proclaim the name of the LORD before thee; and will be gracious to whom I will be gracious, and will shew mercy on whom I will shew mercy. And he said, Thou canst not see my face: for there shall no man see me, and live. And the LORD said, Behold, there is a place by me, and thou shalt stand upon a rock: And it shall come to pass, while my glory passeth by, that I will put thee in a clift of the rock, and will cover thee with my hand while I pass by: And I will take away mine hand, and thou shalt see my back parts: but my face shall not be seen.—Exodus 33:18-23

Moses heard God's voice, saw His shape, and beheld His

glory.ᵉ We will also hear His voice, see His shape, and behold His glory.

> When he shall come to be glorified in his saints, and to be admired in all them that believe (because our testimony among you was believed) in that day.—2 Thessalonians 1:10

Moses watched to see God's glory just as we watch to see God's glory. He saw God's glory only after he was covered by God's hand. God's hand is God's power.² God's power covers us when we are as He is—silent and secret.ᶠ Watching and waiting in the power of His Spirit, until we are wholly in Him, we see God's goodness. He proclaims His name, "I AM." The seen is now the seer.ᵍ We know as we are known. "The whole earth is full of His glory."ʰ

> And the LORD descended in the cloud, and stood with him there, and proclaimed the name of the LORD. And the LORD passed by before him, and proclaimed, The LORD, The LORD God, merciful and gracious, longsuffering, and abundant in goodness and truth, Keeping mercy for thousands, forgiving iniquity and transgression and sin, and that will by no means clear the guilty; visiting the

---

ᵉ And there arose not a prophet since in Israel like unto Moses, whom the LORD knew face to face.—Deuteronomy 34:10; John 5:37; John 8:56

ᶠ When thou prayest, enter into thy closet, and when thou hast shut thy door, pray to thy Father which is in secret; and thy Father which seeth in secret shall reward thee openly.—Matthew 6:6

ᵍ (Beforetime in Israel, when a man went to enquire of God, thus he spake, Come, and let us go to the seer: for he that is now called a Prophet was beforetime called a Seer.)—1 Samuel 9:9

ʰ And one cried unto another, and said, Holy, holy, holy, is the LORD of hosts: the whole earth is full of his glory.—Isaiah 6:3

The Eye Single

iniquity of the fathers upon the children, and upon the children's children, unto the third and to the fourth generation. And Moses made haste, and bowed his head toward the earth, and worshipped.
—Exodus 34:5-8

The Fiery Serpent

THE LORD said unto Moses, Make thee a fiery serpent, and set it upon a pole: and it shall come to pass, that every one that is bitten, when he looketh upon it, shall live.
—Numbers 21:8

Jesus said, "*And as Moses lifted up the serpent in the wilderness, even so must the Son of man be lifted up.*"[1]

> For he hath made him to be sin for us, who knew no sin; that we might be made the righteousness of God in him.—2 Corinthians 5:21

THE EYE SINGLE

Jesus is our fiery serpent. He became sin for us. He took upon Himself the desirous life, which snakes through the spine to pulse in our senses.[2] He exalted life in the flesh, transforming it through obedience in the things that He suffered, even death upon the cross.[a]

> And he said to them all, If any man will come after me, let him deny himself, and take up his cross daily, and follow me.—Luke 9:23

When you watch, you take up your cross; you willingly suspend your carnal nature between heaven and earth where it withers. Watch daily until it dies.

> And he bearing his cross went forth into a place called the place of a skull, which is called in the Hebrew Golgotha: Where they crucified him, and two other with him, on either side one, and Jesus in the midst.—John 19:17-18

All watchers are crucified in "the place of a skull." The two thieves are our two natures, flesh and spirit: one is condemned, the other redeemed.[b]

> Jesus, crying with a loud voice, said, Father, into thy hands I commend my spirit: and having said this, he gave up the ghost. And when the centurion saw what was done, he glorified God, saying,

---

[a] Though he were a Son, yet learned he obedience by the things which he suffered; And being made perfect, he became the author of eternal salvation unto all them that obey him.—Hebrews 5:8-9

[b] And he said unto Jesus, Lord, remember me when thou comest into thy kingdom. And Jesus said unto him, Verily I say unto thee, To day shalt thou be with me in paradise.—Luke 23:42-43

> Certainly this was a righteous man. And all the multitudes that came together to this sight, when they beheld the things that were done, returned smiting their breasts. And all his acquaintance, and the women that followed with him from Galilee, stood afar off, seeing these things.
> —Luke 23:46-49 ASV

"All the multitudes that came together to this sight" watched Jesus' body of flesh die.[c] They watched and waited six hours.[3] Jesus watched with them.

> Knowing this, that our old man is crucified with him, that the body of sin might be destroyed, that henceforth we should not serve sin. For he that is dead is freed from sin. Now if we be dead with Christ, we believe that we shall also live with him.—Romans 6:6-8

---

[c] And sitting down they watched him there.—Matthew 27:36

Standing Still In Jordan

The Lord said unto Joshua, This day will I begin to magnify thee in the sight of all Israel, that they may know that, as I was with Moses, so I will be with thee. And thou shalt command the priests that bear the ark of the covenant, saying, When ye are come to the brink of the water of Jordan, ye shall stand still in Jordan.
—Joshua 3:7-8

Joshua was magnified in the sight of the Israelites as he led them into the Promised Land. Jesus is exalted in the sight of Christians as He leads us into the Kingdom of God. It happens when you and I (the priests), bearing Jesus (the ark of the new covenant),[1] "stand still in Jordan." Jordan means *descender*.[2] The river symbolizes the spirit of life that descends from above.[3]

> And it shall come to pass, as soon as the soles of the feet of the priests that bear the ark of the LORD, the Lord of all the earth, shall rest in the waters of Jordan, that the waters of Jordan shall be cut off from the waters that come down from above; and they shall stand upon an heap. And as they that bare the ark were come unto Jordan, and the feet of the priests that bare the ark were dipped in the brim of the water, (for Jordan over floweth all his banks all the time of harvest), That the waters which came down from above stood and rose up upon an heap very far from the city Adam, that is beside Zaretan: and those that came down toward the sea of the plain, even the salt sea, failed, and were cut off: and the people passed over right against Jericho. —Joshua 3:13-16

Like the waters of the Jordan, which flow into the Dead Sea, man's spirit became a dead sea because of Adam's disobedience. Now, because of Jesus' obedience, the spirit of life is "heaped up," and God-fearing men are saved all the way back to Adam.

> And the priests that bare the ark of the covenant of the LORD stood firm on dry ground in the midst of Jordan, and all the Israelites passed over on dry ground, until all the people were passed clean over Jordan.
> —Joshua 3:17

Watching is standing still on the firm ground of consciousness while in the midst of pure Being. In stillness, the soul crosses over from flesh to spirit. Wait until it passes "clean over."

Loose Thy Shoe

> It came to pass, when Joshua was by Jericho, that he lifted up his eyes and looked, and, behold, there stood a man over against him with his sword drawn in his hand: and Joshua went unto him, and said unto him, Art thou for us, or for our adversaries? Joshua 5:13

God wants to live in you, to share His very life with you. For that to happen, you must be conscious of and conscious in Him. You look to behold. Joshua looked. He "lifted up his eyes" and beheld the Son of man.

> And he said, Nay; but as captain of the host of the LORD am I now come. And Joshua fell on his face to the earth, and did worship, and said unto him, *What saith my lord unto his servant?* And the captain of the LORD'S host said unto Joshua, Loose thy shoe from off thy foot; for the place whereon thou standest is holy. And Joshua did so. —Joshua 5:14-15

You cannot be in the presence of God with your shoes on. Shoes represent your walk in this world, and your shoes are soiled with sin. You cannot know God with your worldly 'understanding.'

> Peter saith unto him, Thou shalt never wash my feet. Jesus answered him, If I wash thee not, thou hast no part with me. —John 13:8

Better to remove your shoes, fall on your face, and worship like Joshua: *"What saith my lord unto his servant?"*

Jericho

God gave the city of Jericho to Joshua and the Israelites, but they had to take it. He told them how:

> Jericho was straitly shut up because of the children of Israel: *none* went out, and none came in. And the LORD said unto Joshua, See, I have given into thine hand Jericho, and the king thereof, and the mighty men of valour. And ye shall compass the city, all ye men of war, and go round about the city once. Thus shalt thou do six days. And seven priests shall bear before the ark seven trumpets of rams' horns: and the seventh day ye shall compass the city seven times, and the priests shall blow with the trumpets. And it shall come to pass, that when they make a long blast with the ram's horn, and when ye hear the sound of the trumpet, all the people shall shout with a great shout; and the wall of the city shall fall down flat, and the people shall ascend up every man straight before him.—Joshua 6:1-5

Watchers prepare the way of the Lord; they "shut up" the city of the soul by watching every day until the seventh day. The life force that flowed outward through the flesh now flows inward to empower the spirit. What was once physical energy is now spiritual energy. As the "seventh day" nears, the body sounds with power. It is the sign to watch night and day, to silently circle the city seven times. Then, get ready. When the trumpet sounds

The Eye Single

long,[a] be ready. Be ready to shout your whole being into the living Word, "Jesus!"[b] Let the Lord fight for you.[c]

> And it came to pass on the seventh day, that they rose early about the dawning of the day, and compassed the city after the same manner seven times: only on that day they compassed the city seven times. And it came to pass at the seventh time, when the priests blew with the trumpets, Joshua said unto the people, Shout; for the LORD hath given you the city. And the city shall be accursed, even it, and all that are therein, to the LORD: only Rahab the harlot shall live, she and all that are with her in the house, because she hid the messengers that we sent. And ye, in any wise keep yourselves from the accursed thing, lest ye make yourselves accursed, when ye take of the accursed thing, and make the camp of Israel a curse, and trouble it. But all the silver, and gold, and vessels of brass and iron, are consecrated unto the LORD: they shall come into the treasury of the LORD. So the people shouted when the priests blew with the trumpets: and it came to pass, when the people heard the sound of the trumpet, and the people shouted with a great shout, that the wall fell down flat, so that the people went up into the city, every man straight before him, and they took the city. And they utterly destroyed all that

---

[a] God is gone up with a shout, the LORD with the sound of a trumpet. —Psalms 47:5

[b] I will also clothe her priests with salvation: and her saints shall shout aloud for joy.—Psalms 132:16

[c] For the LORD your God is he that goeth with you, to fight for you against your enemies, to save you.—Deuteronomy 20:4

was in the city, both man and woman, young and old, and ox, and sheep, and ass, with the edge of the sword.—Joshua 6:15-21

What will it be like when we "shout" through to the Spirit and are caught up to meet the Lord in the air,[4] when we finally see the heavens open and Jesus coming in the clouds?[d] "Old things are passed away; behold, all things are become new."[5] Our souls, once harlots of the body temple,[e] are saved by faith in the "scarlet thread"[f] of the blood of Jesus.[g] Filled with truth and love ("all the silver and gold"), we enter "into the treasury of the LORD."

---

[d] And then shall they see the Son of man coming in the clouds with great power and glory.—Mark 13:26

[e] By faith the harlot Rahab perished not with them that believed not, when she had received the spies with peace.—Hebrews 11:31

[f] Behold, when we come into the land, thou shalt bind this line of scarlet thread in the window which thou didst let us down by: and thou shalt bring thy father, and thy mother, and thy brethren, and all thy father's household, home unto thee. —Joshua 2:18

[g] Having therefore, brethren, boldness to enter into the holiest by the blood of Jesus, By a new and living way, which he hath consecrated for us, through the veil, that is to say, his flesh.—Hebrews 10:19-20

Empty Vessels

THE children of Israel did evil in the sight of the LORD: and the LORD delivered them into the hand of Midian seven years. —Judges 6:1

When the children of Israel cried out to the Lord because of the Midianites, the Lord had mercy and sent a prophet.

> Thus saith the LORD God of Israel, I brought you up from Egypt, and brought you forth out of the house of bondage; And I delivered you out of the hand of the Egyptians, and out of the hand of all that oppressed you, and drave them

> out from before you, and gave you their land;
> And I said unto you, I am the LORD your God;
> fear not the gods of the Amorites, in whose
> land ye dwell: but ye have not obeyed my
> voice. —Judges 6:7-10

Then the Lord sent His angel to commission Gideon to deliver His people. Gideon raised an army of thousands, but that was too many.[1] The Lord told him to send all but three hundred home.[2] It would be three hundred against more than one hundred and thirty thousand.[3] The glory would be the Lord's.

> It came to pass the same night, that the LORD
> said unto him, Arise, get thee down unto the
> host; for I have delivered it into thine hand. But
> if thou fear to go down, go thou with Phurah
> thy servant down to the host: And thou shalt
> hear what they say; and afterward shall thine
> hands be strengthened to go down unto the
> host. Then went he down with Phurah his
> servant unto the outside of the armed men that
> were in the host. —Judges 7:9-11

God speaks in dreams.[4] He wakes us to watch.[5] He woke Gideon and told him to steal into the Midianite camp to hear the telling of a dream and its interpretation:

> When Gideon was come, behold, there was a
> man that told a dream unto his fellow, and
> said, Behold, I dreamed a dream, and, lo, a cake
> of barley bread tumbled into the host of Midian,
> and came unto a tent, and smote it that it fell,
> and overturned it, that the tent lay along. And
> his fellow answered and said, This is nothing

> else save the sword of Gideon the son of Joash, a man of Israel: for into his hand hath God delivered Midian, and all the host.
> —Judges 7:13-14

The Midianites represent the armies of the flesh; the Israelites, the forces of the Spirit. This is the climactic battle. It happens in the watches of the night when men sleep, for sleep is death,[a] and "the last enemy that shall be destroyed is death."[6]

> And it was so, when Gideon heard the telling of the dream, and the interpretation thereof, that he worshipped, and returned into the host of Israel, and said, Arise; for the LORD hath delivered into your hand the host of Midian. And he divided the three hundred men into three companies, and he put a trumpet in every man's hand, with empty pitchers, and lamps within the pitchers. And he said unto them, Look on me, and do likewise: and, behold, when I come to the outside of the camp, it shall be that, as I do, so shall ye do. When I blow with a trumpet, I and all that are with me, then blow ye the trumpets also on every side of all the camp, and say, The sword of the LORD, and of Gideon. So Gideon, and the hundred men that were with him, came unto the outside of the camp in the beginning of the middle watch; and they had but newly set the watch: and they blew the trumpets, and brake the pitchers that were in their hands. And the

---

[a] He said unto them, Give place: for the maid is not dead, but sleepeth. And they laughed him to scorn.—Matthew 9:24; John 11:11-14

> three companies blew the trumpets, and brake the pitchers, and held the lamps in their left hands, and the trumpets in their right hands to blow withal: and they cried, The sword of the LORD, and of Gideon. And they stood every man in his place round about the camp: and all the host ran, and cried, and fled. And the three hundred blew the trumpets, and the LORD set every man's sword against his fellow, even throughout all the host: and the host fled to Bethshittah in Zererath, and to the border of Abelmeholah, unto Tabbath. — Judges 7:15-22

The Israelites overcame the Midianites with empty pitchers, lamps, trumpets, and a shout. Watchers are empty pitchers,[b] and the lamp within a watcher is the eye single.

> The lamp of the body is the eye: if therefore thine eye be single, thy whole body shall be full of light. — Matthew 6:22 ASV

The "trumpet in every man's hand" is the physical body; watching makes it sound. As you persevere in daily watching, power builds in the spiritual body until the force is heard and felt in the physical body. Whenever you hear or feel the power of the Spirit, watch.[c] Watch until you can watch night and day. At the last trumpet, when the trumpet sounds long, join with all your being — shout into God![d]

---

[b] But now, O LORD, thou art our father; we are the clay, and thou our potter; and we all are the work of thy hand. — Isaiah 64:8

[c] That they should seek the Lord, if haply they might feel after him, and find him, though he be not far from every one of us. — Acts 17:27

[d] And Jesus cried with a loud voice, and gave up the ghost. — Mark 15:37

The Eye Single

The host of Israel shouted, "The sword of the LORD, and of Gideon," broke their pitchers, and light streamed forth. The shout gathers all your life force and all your life's breath and blows you into the Spirit; it breaks your earthen vessel. Then stand as the enemy self-destructs. Watch walls tumble, armies flounder. See the firstborn slain. Blow the trumpet! Shout! Break the pitcher. Let light stream forth.

The Double Portion

> BEHOLD, I will send you Elijah the prophet before the coming of the great and dreadful day of the LORD: And he shall turn the heart of the fathers to the children, and the heart of the children to their fathers, lest I come and smite the earth with a curse. —Malachi 4:5-6

Elijah was a 'wild' man. He was a type of the forerunner, John the Baptist,[1] who heralded "the coming of the great and dreadful day of the LORD." The man who seeks God is first an Elijah—a man of God—in whose mouth the word of the Lord is truth.[2]

The 'Elijah-man' abandons the world to enter the wilderness of the soul. The world persecutes him because he aspires to be as his

The Eye Single

Maker, righteous and holy.[a]

> Jesus answered and said unto them, Elias [Elijah] truly shall first come, and restore all things. But I say unto you, That Elias is come already, and they knew him not, but have done unto him whatsoever they listed. Likewise shall also the Son of man suffer of them. Then the disciples understood that he spake unto them of John the Baptist.—Matthew 17:11-13

Elijah's word wielded the power of God. He fed the hungry and raised the dead;[3] he called fire down from heaven[4] and prayed rain on a drought stricken land.[5] Yet, when Jezebel swore to kill him for slaying the prophets of Baal, he fled for his life.

> So let the gods do to me, and more also, if I make not thy life as the life of one of them by to morrow about this time. And when he saw that, he arose, and went for his life, and came to Beersheba, which belongeth to Judah, and left his servant there.—1 Kings 19:2-3

Elijah wanted God to take his life:

> He himself went a day's journey into the wilderness, and came and sat down under a juniper tree: and he requested for himself that he might die; and said, It is enough; now, O Lord, take away my life; for I am not better than my fathers.—1 Kings 19:4

---

[a] Blessed are they which are persecuted for righteousness' sake: for theirs is the kingdom of heaven.—Matthew 5:10

The Lord would indeed take Elijah's life. But first he was to travel to the mountain of God, as Moses had done before, to meet with and see God.[6]

> As he lay and slept under a juniper tree, behold, then an angel touched him, and said unto him, Arise and eat. And he looked, and, behold, there was a cake baken on the coals, and a cruse of water at his head. And he did eat and drink, and laid him down again.—1 Kings 19:5-6

Without sustenance the mountain of God was too far for Elijah, as it is for us. Therefore, "he looked," and "he did eat and drink" what he saw—bread and water from heaven.[b]

> And the angel of the LORD came again the second time, and touched him, and said, Arise and eat; because the journey is too great for thee. And he arose, and did eat and drink, and went in the strength of that meat forty days and forty nights unto Horeb the mount of God.—1 Kings 19:7-8

"In the strength of that meat," Elijah arrived at Horeb, the mountain of God, and lodged in a cave. The "word of the LORD came to him" there, *What doest thou here, Elijah?*[7]

> I have been very jealous for the LORD God of hosts: for the children of Israel have forsaken thy covenant, thrown down thine altars, and

---

[b] Jesus answered and said unto her, If thou knewest the gift of God, and who it is that saith to thee, Give me to drink; thou wouldest have asked of him, and he would have given thee living water.—John 4:10

> slain thy prophets with the sword; and I, even I only, am left; and they seek my life, to take it away. —1 Kings 19:10

Deserted, exiled and alone, Elijah ached for God, and God ached for him. He wanted to see God and be with God, and God wanted to see and be with him.

God said to His faithful servant, *"Go forth, and stand upon the mount before the LORD."*

> And behold, the LORD passed by, and a great and strong wind rent the mountains, and brake in pieces the rocks before the LORD; but the LORD was not in the wind: and after the wind an earthquake; but the LORD was not in the earthquake: And after the earthquake a fire; but the LORD was not in the fire: and after the fire a still small voice. And it was so, when Elijah heard it, that he wrapped his face in his mantle, and went out, and stood in the entering in of the cave. And, behold there came a voice unto him, and said, *What doest thou here, Elijah?*
> —1 Kings 19:11-13

The Lord passed by, but He was not in His effects, not in the wonders and power of nature. Then Elijah heard "a still small voice," and he covered his face with his mantle. God had revealed Himself! Not only was Elijah inside the mountain of God, God was inside him.

> And as they thus spake, Jesus himself stood in the midst of them, and saith unto them, Peace be unto you. But they were terrified and affrighted, and supposed that they had seen a spirit.
> —Luke 24:36-37

Elijah was in the secret place of the Most High, and the Most High was in the heart of man.[8]

> He that dwelleth in the secret place of the most High shall abide under the shadow of the Almighty. —Psalms 91:1

Watchers wrestle with sleep, as did Elijah. We watch, we sleep, and watch again, always rising when called, always eating our portion. We look, and "in the strength of that meat," we journey through the wilderness of the soul to the mountain of God, lodge in the Rock, and hear the "still small voice."

First Elijah, Then Elisha

*A*nd it came to pass, when the LORD would take up Elijah into heaven by a whirlwind, that Elijah went with Elisha from Gilgal. And Elijah said unto Elisha, Tarry here, I pray thee; for the LORD hath sent me to Bethel. —2 Kings 2:1-2

Elijah, at the behest of God, anointed Elisha prophet in his stead.[1] Elisha knew that Elijah was about to ascend to God. He knew he could not let the man of God out of his sight.[a]

---

[a] Then shall two be in the field; the one shall be taken, and the other left. Two women shall be grinding at the mill; the one shall be taken, and the other left. Watch therefore: for ye know not what hour your Lord doth come. —Matthew 24:40-42

> And Elijah said unto him, Elisha, tarry here, I pray thee; for the LORD hath sent me to Jericho. And he [Elisha] said, *As the LORD liveth, and as thy soul liveth, I will not leave thee.* So they came to Jericho. — 2 Kings 2:4

In obedience to God, Elijah and Elisha traversed the cities of the soul.

> After these things the Lord appointed other seventy also, and sent them two and two before his face into every city and place, whither he himself would come. — Luke 10:1

They could not perfect themselves, but they made the way straight.[b]

> But when they persecute you in this city, flee ye into another: for verily I say unto you, ye shall not have gone over the cities of Israel, until the Son of man be come. — Matthew 10:23

Watchers also make the way straight. Like Elijah, we obey; like Elisha, we tarry. When the Son of man comes, He shall perfect you.[c] He shall take Elijah away from your "head" and place him in His heart.

So "hold ye your peace," and stand "to view afar off." You will say with Jesus, "*I beheld Satan as lightning fall from heaven.*"[2]

---

[b] And if thy right eye offend thee, pluck it out, and cast it from thee: for it is profitable for thee that one of thy members should perish, and not that thy whole body should be cast into hell.—Matthew 5:29

[c] But when that which is perfect is come, then that which is in part shall be done away.—1 Corinthians 13:10; Luke 10:1

The Eye Single

> And the sons of the prophets that were at Jericho came to Elisha, and said unto him, Knowest thou that the LORD will take away thy master from thy head to day? And he answered, Yea, I know it; hold ye your peace. And Elijah said unto him, Tarry, I pray thee, here; for the LORD hath sent me to Jordan. And he said, As the LORD liveth, and as thy soul liveth, I will not leave thee. And they two went on. And fifty men of the sons of the prophets went, and stood to view afar off: and they two stood by Jordan. —2 Kings 2:5-7

Elisha was determined to witness Elijah's ascension. Not since God took Enoch had a man been translated into heaven.[d] Why would Elijah not want Elisha to witness his 'catching away'—his rapture![3]

> And ye shall seek me, and find me, when ye shall search for me with all your heart. And I will be found of you, saith the LORD.
> —Jeremiah 29:12-14

Like Jacob, Elisha clung to the man of God. He would not let go until he was blessed with the new nature.

> Elijah took his mantle, and wrapped it together, and smote the waters, and they were divided hither and thither, so that they two went over on dry ground. —2 Kings 2:8

"When they were gone over," Elijah said to Elisha, "*Ask what I shall do for thee, before I be taken away from thee.*"

---

[d] And Enoch walked with God: and he was not; for God took him.—Genesis 5:24

Elisha answered, "*I pray thee, let a double portion of thy spirit be upon me.*"

Elijah then said, "*Thou hast asked a hard thing: nevertheless, if thou see me when I am taken from thee, it shall be so unto thee; but if not, it shall not be so.*"[4]

For Elisha to receive the double portion, he had to be watching when Elijah—the man of God—was taken.

> And it came to pass, as they still went on, and talked, that, behold, there appeared a chariot of fire, and horses of fire, and parted them both asunder; and Elijah went up by a whirlwind into heaven. And Elisha saw it, and he cried, My father, my father, the chariot of Israel, and the horsemen thereof. And he saw him no more: and he took hold of his own clothes, and rent them in two pieces. He took up also the mantle of Elijah that fell from him, and went back, and stood by the bank of Jordan; And he took the mantle of Elijah that fell from him, and smote the waters, and said, Where is the LORD God of Elijah? and when he also had smitten the waters, they parted hither and thither: and Elisha went over.—2 Kings 2:11-14

Elisha took up Elijah's mantle (he was conscious in the Spirit).[e] He went to the river that descends from on high and "smote the waters" (he wielded the power of God). He "went over" (to the kingdom of God).

> For the kingdom of God is not in word, but in power.—1 Corinthians 4:20

---

[e] And Elisha prayed, and said, LORD, I pray thee, open his eyes, that he may see. And the LORD opened the eyes of the young man; and he saw: and, behold, the mountain was full of horses and chariots of fire round about Elisha.—2 Kings 6:17

The Eye Single

"Where is the LORD God of Elijah?" He is in Elisha! Where is Elijah? He is in God.

> When the sons of the prophets which were to view at Jericho saw him, they said, The spirit of Elijah doth rest on Elisha. And they came to meet him, and bowed themselves to the ground before him. —2 Kings 2:15

It is the same for you. Like Elisha, you continue your life's journey not knowing the day or the hour when Jesus will return for your spirit man. But you will know when the moment nears. Your spirit will be on fire, like a chariot and horses of fire, before a whirlwind of power separates spirit from flesh (your clothing is rent in two), and the Man of God within you ascends to where He was before.[5]

> Who hath ascended up into heaven, or descended?
> Who hath gathered the wind in his fists?
> Who hath bound the waters in a garment?
> Who hath established all the ends of the earth?
> What is his name, and what is his son's name?
> If thou canst tell!
> —Proverbs 30:4

You will see Jesus when you are one with Him, when you are as He is: wholly open to and observant of the spirit, mind, and heart of God. You will see Him and ascend with Him. You will be with Him forevermore.

I Know My Redeemer Liveth

WHAT is man, that You should magnify him, and that You should set Your heart on him, and visit him every morning, trying him every moment? How long will You not look away from me, nor leave me alone until I swallow down my spittle? I have sinned; what do I do to You, O Watcher of man? Why have You set me as a target for You, so that I am a burden on myself?
—Job 7:17-20 LITV

Job was a righteous man who loved and feared God. Yet God allowed Satan, in a cruel test of Job's faithfulness, to plunder his property and slay his servants and children! When messengers brought word of the atrocities:

> Job arose, and rent his mantle, and shaved his head, and fell down upon the ground, and worshipped, And said, Naked came I out of my mother's womb, and naked shall I return thither: the LORD gave, and the LORD hath taken away; blessed be the name of the LORD. —Job 1:20-21

Job didn't curse God, he worshipped! He worshipped the creator, the source and sustainer of all life. But his ordeal wasn't over. It got worse:

> The LORD said unto Satan, Hast thou considered my servant Job, that there is none like him in the earth, a perfect and an upright man, one that feareth God, and escheweth evil? and still he holdeth fast his integrity, although thou movedst me against him, to destroy him without cause. And Satan answered the LORD, and said, Skin for skin, yea, all that a man hath will he give for his life. But put forth thine hand now, and touch his bone and his flesh, and he will curse thee to thy face. And the LORD said unto Satan, Behold, he is in thine hand; but save his life. So went Satan forth from the presence of the LORD, and smote Job with sore boils from the sole of his foot unto his crown. And he took him a pot-sherd to scrape himself withal; and he sat down among the ashes. —Job 2:3-8

Then his wife derided him:

> Dost thou still retain thine integrity? curse God, and die. But he said unto her, Thou speakest as

> one of the foolish women speaketh. What? shall we receive good at the hand of God, and shall we not receive evil? In all this did not Job sin with his lips. —Job 2:9-10

Even his friends assailed him. Though they came to console him, they ended up accusing him, for while Job bewailed his calamity, he maintained his innocence. He wasn't responsible for the evil that had befallen him—God was. God had allowed it, and only God knew why.

> Though he slay me, yet will I trust in him: but I will maintain mine own ways before him. —Job 13:15

To Job's friends, this was blasphemous. Would God destroy a good man? Was Job more righteous than God? Was Job just? No, no, and no. God is good, He is righteous, and He alone is just. Job was getting what he deserved.

> How long wilt thou speak these things? and how long shall the words of thy mouth be like a strong wind? Doth God pervert judgment? or doth the Almighty pervert justice? If thy children have sinned against him, and he have cast them away for their transgression; If thou wouldest seek unto God betimes, and make thy supplication to the Almighty; If thou wert pure and upright; surely now he would awake for thee, and make the habitation of thy righteousness prosperous. —Job 8:1-6

Job answered:

> Have pity upon me, have pity upon me, O ye my friends; for the hand of God hath touched

me. Why do ye persecute me as God, and are not satisfied with my flesh? —Job 19:21-22

After Theophany, Epiphany, Apotheosis

Why did God allow Satan to torment Job? Was it Satan's taunt?

> Skin for skin, yea, all that a man hath will he give for his life. But put forth thine hand now, and touch his bone and his flesh, and he will curse thee to thy face. —Job 2:4-5

Surely not. And what about us? The righteous and holy suffer still. The Lord said to Peter:

> Simon, Simon, behold, Satan hath desired to have you, that he may sift you as wheat: But I have prayed for thee, that thy faith fail not: and when thou art converted, strengthen thy brethren. —Luke 22:31-32

Later, Peter wrote:

> Forasmuch then as Christ hath suffered for us in the flesh, arm yourselves likewise with the same mind: for he that hath suffered in the flesh hath ceased from sin; That he no longer should live the rest of his time in the flesh to the lusts of men, but to the will of God.
> —1 Peter 4:1-2

Paul explains:

> The Spirit itself beareth witness with our spirit, that we are the children of God: And if children,

> then heirs; heirs of God, and joint-heirs with Christ; if so be that we suffer with him, that we may be also glorified together. For I reckon that the sufferings of this present time are not worthy to be compared with the glory which shall be revealed in us. For the earnest expectation of the creature waiteth for the manifestation of the sons of God. For the creature was made subject to vanity, not willingly, but by reason of him who hath subjected the same in hope, Because the creature itself also shall be delivered from the bondage of corruption into the glorious liberty of the children of God. For we know that the whole creation groaneth and travaileth in pain together until now. And not only they, but ourselves also, which have the firstfruits of the Spirit, even we ourselves groan within ourselves, waiting for the adoption, to wit, the redemption of our body.
> —Romans 8:16-23

Job's friends thought God was content with good and obedient worshipers. They were wrong.[1] God wants more.

> So likewise ye, when ye shall have done all those things which are commanded you, say, We are unprofitable servants: we have done that which was our duty to do.—Luke 17:10

God wants us; He wants kinship.

> Having predestinated us unto the adoption of children by Jesus Christ to himself, according to the good pleasure of his will.—Ephesians 1:5

Suffering births children of God. Job suffered because God

wanted him for a son. Hear the words with which Job answered the Lord God:

> *I know that thou canst do all things,*
> *And that no purpose of thine can be restrained.*
> *Who is this that hideth counsel without knowledge?*
> *Therefore have I uttered that which I understood not,*
> *Things too wonderful for me, which I knew not.*
> *Hear, I beseech thee, and I will speak;*
> *I will demand of thee, and declare thou unto me.*
> *I had heard of thee by the hearing of the ear;*
> *But now my eye seeth thee:*
> *Wherefore I abhor myself,*
> *And repent in dust and ashes.*
> —Job 42:1-6 ASV

Job saw the One "in whose hand is the soul of every living thing, and the breath of all mankind."[2] He saw the one in whom "we live, and move, and have our being."[3] He saw I AM; he saw His glory. He saw the "back parts" of God.[4] He saw Him from the inside out. His soul experienced God's soul.[a] He knew what Paul knew:

> I am crucified with Christ: nevertheless I live; yet not I, but Christ liveth in me: and the life which I now live in the flesh I live by the faith of the Son of God, who loved me, and gave himself for me. —Galatians 2:20

Job saw God. "*But now mine eye seeth thee.*" He saw the One living within him. He had prophesied He would see God, and he did:

---

[a] And I will set my tabernacle among you: and my soul shall not abhor you. —Leviticus 26:11

> *Oh that my words were now written!*
> *Oh that they were printed in a book!*
> *That they were graven with an iron pen and lead in the rock for ever!*
> *For I know that my redeemer liveth, and that he shall stand at the latter day upon the earth:*
> *And though after my skin worms destroy this body, yet in my flesh shall I see God:*
> *Whom I shall see for myself, and mine eyes shall behold, and not another; though my reins be consumed within me.*
> —Job 19:23-27

For keeping faith in a good and providential God and maintaining his righteousness in the midst of suffering, Job was granted the beatific vision. The moment he saw the Lord God, his suffering was over, and "the LORD blessed the latter end of Job more than his beginning."[5]

Like Job, watchers suffer the loss of all things that they might see Jesus.

> A little while, and the world seeth me no more; but ye see me: because I live, ye shall live also. At that day ye shall know that I am in my Father, and ye in me, and I in you. —John 14:19-20

Watchers differ in that they suffer of their own volition. They lay down their lives that they might take them up again.

> Therefore doth my Father love me, because I lay down my life, that I might take it again.
> —John 10:17

Comes My Beloved

I AM my beloved's, and his desire is toward me. —Song of Solomon 7:10

Jesus desires those who desire Him, who desire love, who desire Him as the Shulamite desired Solomon.

> Let him kiss me with the kisses of his mouth:
> for thy love is better than wine.
> —Song of Solomon 1:2

The Lord is the love of the heart and the light of the soul. He is love for those who look for Him.

> Behold, thou art fair, my love; behold, thou art
> fair; thou hast doves' eyes.
> —Song of Solomon 1:15

As a rose of Sharon or a lily of the valley,[1] bask in the light of the Son.

> As the lily among thorns, so is my love among
> the daughters.—Song of Solomon 2:2

Your Lord is the tree of life. His fruit is peace, love and joy.[a]

> As the apple tree among the trees of the wood,
> so is my beloved among the sons. I sat down
> under his shadow with great delight, and his
> fruit was sweet to my taste.
> —Song of Solomon 2:3

He will bring you to His banqueting house and comfort you with love.

> He brought me to the banqueting house, and
> his banner over me was love. Stay me with
> flagons, comfort me with apples: for I am sick
> of love.—Song of Solomon 2:4-5

If you are "sick of love," wait for love. Love comes when He wills.

> His left hand is under my head, and his right
> hand doth embrace me. I charge you, O ye

---

[a] But the fruit of the Spirit is love, joy, peace, longsuffering, gentleness, goodness, faith, meekness, temperance: against such there is no law.—Galatians 5:22-23

> daughters of Jerusalem, by the roes, and by the hinds of the field, that ye stir not up, nor awake my love, till he please.
> —Song of Solomon 2:6-7

Listen for the voice of the beloved. "Behold, he cometh leaping upon the mountains, skipping upon the hills."

> He standeth behind our wall, he looketh forth at the windows, shewing himself through the lattice. —Song of Solomon 2:8-9

He calls:

> Rise up, my love, my fair one, and come away. For, lo, the winter is past, the rain is over and gone; The flowers appear on the earth; the time of the singing of birds is come, and the voice of the turtle is heard in our land; The fig tree putteth forth her green figs, and the vines with the tender grape give a good smell. Arise, my love, my fair one, and come away.
> —Song of Solomon 2:10-13

Embrace Him in the secret place.

> Arise, my love, my fair one, and come away. O my dove, that art in the clefts of the rock, in the secret places of the stairs, let me see thy countenance, let me hear thy voice; for sweet is thy voice, and thy countenance is comely.
> —Song of Solomon 2:13-14

Cling to Him "until the day breathes and the shadows flee."

> My beloved is mine, and I am his; he grazes among the lilies. Until the day breathes and the shadows flee, turn, my beloved, be like a gazelle or a young stag on cleft mountains.
> —Song of Solomon 2:16-17 ESV

Seek Him by night. Seek the One whom your "soul loveth."

> I remember thee upon my bed, and meditate on thee in the night watches. —Psalms 63:5-6

Seek Him until you find Him. Bring Him into your "mother's house, and into the chamber of her that conceived" you.

> By night on my bed I sought him whom my soul loveth: I sought him, but I found him not. I will rise now, and go about the city in the streets, and in the broad ways I will seek him whom my soul loveth: I sought him, but I found him not. The watchmen that go about the city found me: to whom I said, Saw ye him whom my soul loveth? It was but a little that I passed from them, but I found him whom my soul loveth: I held him, and would not let him go, until I had brought him into my mother's house, and into the chamber of her that conceived me. —Song of Solomon 3:1-4

When He wakes you, arise. When He calls, let Him in.

> I sleep, but my heart waketh: it is the voice of my beloved that knocketh, saying, Open to me, my sister, my love, my dove, my undefiled: for my head is filled with dew, and my locks with

> the drops of the night. I have put off my coat; how shall I put it on? I have washed my feet; how shall I defile them? My beloved put in his hand by the hole of the door, and my bowels were moved for him. I rose up to open to my beloved; and my hands dropped with myrrh, and my fingers with sweet smelling myrrh, upon the handles of the lock. I opened to my beloved; but my beloved had withdrawn himself, and was gone: my soul failed when he spake: I sought him, but I could not find him; I called him, but he gave me no answer. The watchmen that went about the city found me, they smote me, they wounded me; the keepers of the walls took away my veil from me.
> —Song of Solomon 5:2-7

If you miss Him, search for Him. Your eyes overcome Him.

> Thou art beautiful, O my love, as Tirzah, comely as Jerusalem, terrible as an army with banners. Turn away thine eyes from me, for they have overcome me: thy hair is as a flock of goats that appear from Gilead.
> —Song of Solomon 6:4-5

Love Him as He loves you—with your whole heart. Draw nigh unto Him, and He will draw nigh unto you.[b] Pray the Father to see the Son.[c]

---

[b] Draw nigh to God, and he will draw nigh to you. Cleanse your hands, ye sinners; and purify your hearts, ye double minded.—James 4:8

[c] And I will pray the Father, and he shall give you another Comforter, that he may abide with you for ever.—John 14:16

> No man can come to me, except the Father which hath sent me draw him: and I will raise him up at the last day. —John 6:44

"Come, Lord Jesus."[2]

> Make haste, my beloved, and be thou like to a roe or to a young hart upon the mountains of spices. —Song of Solomon 8:14

I watch to see,
In Galilee,
Darkness,
Death enclose me.
I wait to see
Light spring up,
Born of God,
His Kingdom come—
Power,
Glory,
Amen.

I am the light of the world:
he that followeth me shall
not walk in darkness, but shall
have the light of life.

John 8:12

THE BRIGHT AND MORNING STAR

The Messenger
The Watchman
The Kingdom Of God

The Messenger

THERE was a man sent from God, whose name was John. The same came for a witness, to bear witness of the Light, that all men through him might believe. —John 1:6-7

John was born to the priest Zacharias and Elisabeth his wife, who was a cousin of Mary.[1] He was a child of promise and "great in the sight of the Lord."

> The angel said unto him, Fear not, Zacharias: for thy prayer is heard; and thy wife Elisabeth shall bear thee a son, and thou shalt call his name

> John. And thou shalt have joy and gladness; and many shall rejoice at his birth. For he shall be great in the sight of the Lord, and shall drink neither wine nor strong drink; and he shall be filled with the Holy Ghost, even from his mother's womb.—Luke 1:13-15

Christians are also children of promise.[a] Born of God our Father, we too are filled with the Holy Ghost, even from our Mother's womb.[b]

> Born, not of blood, nor of the will of the flesh, nor of the will of man, but of God.—John 1:13

John watched for the One who baptizes with the Holy Ghost and fire.[2] He looked for Him in a stark and desolate land. The "word of God" came to him there,[3] and he became "a burning and a shining light."[4]

> Thou, child, shalt be called the prophet of the Highest: for thou shalt go before the face of the Lord to prepare his ways; To give knowledge of salvation unto his people by the remission of their sins, Through the tender mercy of our God; whereby the dayspring from on high hath visited us, To give light to them that sit in darkness and in the shadow of death, to guide our feet into the way of peace. And the child grew, and waxed strong in spirit, and was in the deserts till the day of his shewing unto Israel.—Luke 1:76-80

---

[a] Now we, brethren, as Isaac was, are the children of promise.—Galatians 4:28; Genesis 17:19

[b] So God created man in his own image, in the image of god created he him; male and female created he them.—Genesis 1:27

The Eye Single

In John, Christ Forms

> I am the voice of one crying in the wilderness, Make straight the way of the Lord, as said the prophet Esaias. —John 1:23

John preached the baptism of repentance for the remission of sins,[5] *"Repent ye: for the kingdom of heaven is at hand.[6] Bring forth therefore fruits worthy of repentance."*[7]

The people asked, *"What shall we do then?"*

John answered, *"He that hath two coats, let him impart to him that hath none; and he that hath meat, let him do likewise."*

The tax collectors asked, *"Master, what shall we do?"*

He replied, *"Exact no more than that which is appointed you."*

The soldiers demanded, *"What shall we do?"*

To them he added, *"Do violence to no man, neither accuse any falsely; and be content with your wages."*[8]

> Then cometh Jesus from Galilee to Jordan unto John, to be baptized of him. But John forbad him, saying, I have need to be baptized of thee, and comest thou to me? And Jesus answering said unto him, Suffer it to be so now: for thus it becometh us to fulfil all righteousness. Then he suffered him. —Matthew 3:13-15

Jesus came to be "born of water and of the Spirit."

> Verily, verily, I say unto thee, Except a man be born of water and of the Spirit, he cannot enter into the kingdom of God. —John 3:5

When He was baptized, He:

> Went up straightway out of the water: and, lo,

> the heavens were opened unto him, and he saw the Spirit of God descending like a dove, and lighting upon him: And lo a voice from heaven, saying, This is my beloved Son, in whom I am well pleased. —Matthew 3:16-17

All must prepare the way of the Lord.[c] All must be as righteous as John,[9] and each one of us must be "in the deserts until the day of his shewing unto Israel."[d] Remain in the deserts until the Word of God comes to you. Let Jesus form within. Watch, and the child grows, waxing strong in spirit. Wait, "and the Lord, whom ye seek, shall suddenly come to his temple."

> Behold, I will send my messenger, and he shall prepare the way before me: and the Lord, whom ye seek, shall suddenly come to his temple, even the messenger of the covenant, whom ye delight in: behold, he shall come, saith the LORD of hosts. —Malachi 3:1

"Fulfill all righteousness" by birthing Jesus into your life.

> Know ye not, that so many of us as were baptized into Jesus Christ were baptized into his death? Therefore we are buried with him by baptism into death: that like as Christ was raised up from the dead by the glory of the Father, even so we also should walk in newness of life.
> —Romans 6:3-4

---

[c] Follow peace with all men, and holiness, without which no man shall see the LORD.—Hebrews 12:14

[d] It is written in the prophets, Behold, I send my messenger before thy face, which shall prepare thy way before thee. The voice of one crying in the wilderness, Prepare ye the way of the Lord, make his paths straight.—Mark 1:2-3

The Eye Single

First Death, Then Life

> If the world hate you, ye know that it hated me before it hated you. If ye were of the world, the world would love his own: but because ye are not of the world, but I have chosen you out of the world, therefore the world hateth you.
> —John 15:18-19

John separated himself from the world. He did not move to the dance of desire. He condemned the flesh man (Herod) and embraced the spirit man (Jesus). When he reproved Herod for his unlawful marriage to Herodias (his sister-in-law),[10] Herod cast John into prison where he sat in darkness, "in the region and shadow of death."

> When Jesus had heard that John was cast into prison, he departed into Galilee; And leaving Nazareth, he came and dwelt in Capernaum, which is upon the sea coast, in the borders of Zabulon and Nephthalim: That it might be fulfilled which was spoken by Esaias the prophet, saying, The land of Zabulon, and the land of Nephthalim, by the way of the sea, beyond Jordan, Galilee of the Gentiles; The people which sat in darkness saw great light; and to them which sat in the region and shadow of death light is sprung up.—Matthew 4:12-16

Herodias hated John and "would have killed him, but she could not, for Herod feared John." Herod feared John as a holy man, "heard him gladly" and tried to please him,[11] yet he would not cut himself off from his evil, scheming wife.

When Herod's birthday was kept, the daughter

> of Herodias danced before them, and pleased Herod. Whereupon he promised with an oath to give her whatsoever she would ask. And she, being before instructed of her mother, said, Give me here John Baptist's head in a charger. And the king was sorry: nevertheless for the oath's sake, and them which sat with him at meat, he commanded it to be given her. And he sent, and beheaded John in the prison. And his head was brought in a charger, and given to the damsel: and she brought it to her mother. —Matthew 14:6-11

After John's beheading:

> His disciples came, and took up the body, and buried it, and went and told Jesus. When Jesus heard of it, he departed thence by ship into a desert place apart: and when the people had heard thereof, they followed him on foot out of the cities. —Matthew 14:12-13

Leave the earthly city for the heavenly. Find Him "in a desert place apart." When John dies, Jesus lives.

> He must increase, but I must decrease. He that cometh from above is above all: he that is of the earth is earthly, and speaketh of the earth: he that cometh from heaven is above all. —John 3:30-31

Jesus said:

> From the days of John the Baptist until now the kingdom of heaven suffereth violence, and the violent take it by force. —Matthew 11:12

The Eye Single

Take the kingdom of heaven by force. Kill your flesh man!

> And if Christ be in you, the body is dead because of sin; but the Spirit is life because of righteousness. — Romans 8:10

Let the spirit man live.

> At that time Herod the tetrarch heard of the fame of Jesus, And said unto his servants, This is John the Baptist; he is risen from the dead; and therefore mighty works do shew forth themselves in him. — Matthew 14:1-2

The Watchman

*I*N the sixth month the angel Gabriel was sent from God unto a city of Galilee, named Nazareth, To a virgin espoused to a man whose name was Joseph, of the house of David; and the virgin's name was Mary. — Luke 1:26-27

The city of Nazareth[1] was a watchtower situated in hills that overlooked important trade routes. God became man in Nazareth. Jesus was conceived in Nazareth, born in Bethlehem, found refuge in Egypt, and "came and dwelt in a city called Nazareth: that it might be fulfilled which was spoken by the prophets, He shall be called a Nazarene."[2]

The Eye Single

"Jesus of Nazareth" is mentioned twelve times in the Gospels and five times in the book of *Acts*. Pilate wrote "JESUS OF NAZARETH THE KING OF THE JEWS" and put it on the cross.[3]

Paul asked, "*Who art thou, Lord?*"

Our Lord replied, "*I am Jesus of Nazareth, whom thou persecutest.*"[4]

Jesus of Nazareth, the Nazarene, was a watchman from the watchtower, a watcher like His Father, whom Job called the "watcher of man."[5] The followers of the Nazarene, watchers like their Master, were called "the sect of the Nazarenes."[6]

> Son of man, I have made thee a watchman unto the house of Israel: therefore hear the word at my mouth, and give them warning from me.
> —Ezekiel 3:17

Come And See

After His temptation in the wilderness, Jesus returned in the power of the Spirit.[7] John the Baptist pointed Him out to two of his disciples as He walked by saying, "*Behold the Lamb of God!*"

The two disciples of John followed Jesus and asked, "*Where dwellest thou?*"

Jesus answered, "*Come and see.*"

They went with Him "and saw where he dwelt, and abode with him that day: for it was about the tenth hour."[8]

Soon after, Jesus went to Galilee, He found Philip and said, "*Follow me.*"[9]

Afterwards, Philip sought out Nathanael and announced: "*We have found him, of whom Moses in the law, and the prophets, did write, Jesus of Nazareth, the son of Joseph.*"

Nathanael replied, "*Can there any good thing come out of Nazareth?*"

Philip said, "*Come and see.*"[10]

Come and see the one who "dwelleth not in temples made with hands,"[11] who dwells "in the light which no man can approach unto; whom no man hath seen, nor can see."[12] Come and see. It is the tenth hour: "The time is fulfilled, and the kingdom of God is at hand."[13] Come and see.

THE KINGDOM OF GOD

JESUS came into Galilee, preaching the gospel of the kingdom of God, And saying, The time is fulfilled, and the kingdom of God is at hand: repent ye, and believe the gospel. — Mark 1:14-15

The kingdom of God is the rule of God in your life. It is "righteousness, peace, and joy in the Holy Ghost."[1] It is "not in word, but in power."[2]

> But if I with the finger of God cast out devils, no doubt the kingdom of God is come upon you.
> —Luke 11:20

The kingdom of God is God's will done on earth as it is in heaven.³ It's good news because God's will is good. Jesus said:

> *Why callest thou me good? none is good, save one, that is, God.* —Luke 18:19

His goodness is His glory.

> If ye abide in me, and my words abide in you, ye shall ask what ye will, and it shall be done unto you. Herein is my Father glorified, that ye bear much fruit; so shall ye be my disciples.
> —John 15:7-8

"*Seek ye the kingdom of God,*" commanded Jesus.⁴ He gave simple, straightforward instructions:

> Fear not, little flock; for it is your Father's good pleasure to give you the kingdom. Sell that ye have, and give alms; provide yourselves bags which wax not old, a treasure in the heavens that faileth not, where no thief approacheth, neither moth corrupteth. For where your treasure is, there will your heart be also. Let your loins be girded about, and your lights burning; And ye your-selves like unto men that wait for their Lord, when he will return from the wedding; that when he cometh and knocketh, they may open unto him immediately.
> —Luke 12:32-36

The first thing to do to receive the kingdom is: "Sell that ye have, and give alms." Do this and you will "love the Lord thy God with all thy heart, and with all thy soul, and with all thy mind, and with all thy strength."[5] "For where your treasure is, there will your heart be also."

Once your heart is in heaven, watch for your Lord's return. Gird yourself. Keep the lids off the lamps and "your lights burning." Look for Him night and day. If Jesus finds you watching, He will come forth and serve you!

> Blessed are those servants, whom the Lord when he cometh shall find watching: verily I say unto you, that he shall gird himself, and make them to sit down to meat, and will come forth and serve them. — Luke 12:37

The kingdom of God is your inheritance. It has been prepared for you from the foundation of the world.

> Then shall the King say unto them on his right hand, Come, ye blessed of my Father, inherit the kingdom prepared for you from the foundation of the world. — Matthew 25:34

The Son of God died that you might receive it, but it is taken by force.[6] The force required is secured by watching daily. Watch every day, and you will begin to hear and feel the sounding power of Spirit.

> So is the kingdom of God, as if a man should cast seed into the ground; And should sleep, and rise night and day, and the seed should spring and grow up, he knoweth not how. For the earth bringeth forth fruit of herself; first the blade, then the ear, after that the full corn

> in the ear. But when the fruit is brought forth, immediately he putteth in the sickle, because the harvest is come. — Mark 4:26-29

When you experience a crescendo of power, Jesus is about to appear.

> He shall send his angels with a great sound of a trumpet, and they shall gather together his elect from the four winds, from one end of heaven to the other. — Matthew 24:31

Whenever the Spirit moves you to watch — whether night or day — watch.

> Surely I will not come into the tabernacle of my house, nor go up into my bed; I will not give sleep to mine eyes, or slumber to mine eyelids, Until I find out a place for the LORD, an habitation for the mighty God of Jacob.
> — Psalms 132:3-5

If you are found watching when Jesus returns, nothing can prevent you from receiving His kingdom and sharing His glory: "Ye shall receive a crown of glory that fadeth not away."[7]

> When Christ, who is our life, shall appear, then shall ye also appear with him in glory.
> — Colossians 3:4

Go And See In Galilee

Jesus came "to give light to them that sit in darkness and in the shadow of death."[8] He came to "Galilee of the gentiles."[9]

> The people which sat in darkness saw great light; and to them which sat in the region and shadow of death light is sprung up.
> —Matthew 4:16

Jesus told His disciples:

> After I am risen again, I will go before you into Galilee. —Matthew 26:32

The angel of the Lord who rolled back the stone from the entrance of the tomb told "Mary Magdalene[10] and the other Mary,"[11] who had come to the sepulcher:

> Behold, he goeth before you into Galilee; there shall ye see him: lo, I have told you.
> —Matthew 28:1-7

The excited women ran to tell the disciples but stopped when Jesus suddenly appeared before them and said:

> Be not afraid: Go tell my brethren that they go into Galilee, and there shall they see me.
> —Matthew 28:10

Jesus ascended to heaven from Galilee, and the brethren watched as "a cloud received Him out of their sight."

> And while they looked stedfastly toward heaven as he went up, behold, two men stood by them in white apparel; Which also said, Ye men of Galilee, why stand ye gazing up into heaven? this same Jesus, which is taken up from you into heaven, shall so come in like manner as ye have seen him go into heaven. —Acts 1:9-11

"*Be not afraid.*"[a] Go and see in Galilee. Sit in darkness, "in the region and shadow of death." Wait until "light is sprung up." Gaze into heaven.

---

[a] Fear keeps the baby away and in heaven forever.

I watch!
In light streaming—
The Bright Morning Star.
I wait!
For the perfecting,
The instance,
Of the becoming
In me
Of Thee.

I wait for the LORD,
my soul doth wait,
and in His ward do I hope.
My soul waitheth for the LORD more
than they that watch for the morning:
I say, more than they that
watch for the morning.

Psalm 130:6

THE QUICKENING SPIRIT

In The Image Of Him
Celestial Bodies
In My Father's House
Neither The Day Nor The Hour
Commanding Faith

In The Image Of Him

*T*HE angel answered and said unto her, The Holy Ghost shall come upon thee, and the power of the Highest shall overshadow thee: therefore also that holy thing which shall be born of thee shall be called the Son of God.
—Luke 1:35

Jesus said we must be "born from above."[1] When we accept Jesus as Savior, a spiritual child is conceived within us. As we obey Jesus, the child forms.[a] We wait and watch for His birth in

---

[a] My little children, of whom I travail in birth again until Christ be formed in you. —Galatians 4:19

us, "for the adoption, to wit, the redemption of our body."

> We know that the whole creation groaneth and travaileth in pain together until now. And not only they, but ourselves also, which have the firstfruits of the Spirit, even we ourselves groan within ourselves, waiting for the adoption, to wit, the redemption of our body.
> —Romans 8:22-23

Paul calls "that holy thing which shall be born of thee" the "new man." The new man is "renewed in knowledge after the image of him that created him."[2]

> Be renewed in the spirit of your mind; And that ye put on the new man, which after God is created in righteousness and true holiness.
> —Ephesians 4:23-24

The new man is a spirit man.

> That which is born of the flesh is flesh; and that which is born of the Spirit is spirit.—John 3:6

He "cannot sin."

> Whosoever is born of God doth not commit sin; for his seed remaineth in him: and he cannot sin, because he is born of God.—1 John 3:9

He is "the Lord from heaven."

> The first man is of the earth, earthy: the second man is the Lord from heaven.
> —1 Corinthians 15:47

The Eye Single

Children Of Light

> While ye have light, believe in the light, that ye may be the children of light. —John 12:36

Jesus took Peter, James and John, and "went up into a mountain to pray."

> And as he prayed, the fashion of his countenance was altered, and his raiment was white and glistering. And, behold, there talked with him two men, which were Moses and Elias: Who appeared in glory, and spake of his decease which he should accomplish at Jerusalem. But Peter and they that were with him were heavy with sleep: and when they were awake, they saw his glory, and the two men that stood with him. And it came to pass, as they departed from him, Peter said unto Jesus, Master, it is good for us to be here: and let us make three tabernacles; one for thee, and one for Moses, and one for Elias: not knowing what he said. While he thus spake, there came a cloud, and overshadowed them: and they feared as they entered into the cloud. And there came a voice out of the cloud, saying, This is my beloved Son: hear him. —Luke 9:28-35

The three disciples fell asleep only to awaken in the spirit and witness Jesus speaking with Moses and Elijah, "who appeared in glory." Peter wanted to build tabernacles, but our Father enveloped them with His cloud and said, *"This is my beloved Son: hear him."*

And we have seen and do testify that the Father

> sent the son to be the saviour of the world. Whosoever shall confess that Jesus is the Son of God, God dwelleth in him, and he in God.
> —1 John 4:15

Faithful And Wise Stewards

> Who then is that faithful and wise steward, whom his Lord shall make ruler over his household, to give them their portion of meat in due season? Blessed is that servant, whom his Lord when he cometh shall find so doing. Of a truth I say unto you, that he will make him ruler over all that he hath.—Luke 12:42-44

You are God's household. You are His steward. You are to be a living sacrifice foregoing the pleasure of the flesh for the treasure of the Spirit.[b]

> For our conversation is in heaven; from whence also we look for the Saviour, the Lord Jesus Christ: Who shall change our vile body, that it may be fashioned like unto his glorious body, according to the working whereby he is able even to subdue all things unto himself.
> —Philippians 3:20-21

Stephen

> And then shall they see the Son of man coming in a cloud with power and great glory.
> —Luke 21:27

---

[b] And be not drunk with wine, wherein is excess; but be filled with the Spirit. —Ephesians 5:18

The Eye Single

Stephen exemplified the faithful and wise steward, for he was made ruler over the Lord's "household to give them their portion of meat in due season,"[3] and he was about his Lord's business when his Master returned. He "looked up steadfastly into heaven and saw the glory of God, and Jesus standing on the right hand of God."[4]

Stephen is first mentioned in *Acts* as a man of "honest report, full of the Holy Ghost and wisdom,"[5] who, "full of faith and power, did great wonders and miracles among the people."[6] When the Jews "were not able to resist the wisdom and the spirit by which he spake,"[7] they brought him before the council and accused him of blasphemy.[8]

> And all that sat in the council, looking steadfastly on him, saw his face as it had been the face of an angel. — Acts 6:15

The high priest said, *"Are these things so?"*[9]

Stephen answered by reminding them of their rebellious history with God. His final words were an indictment:

> Ye stiffnecked and uncircumcised in heart and ears, ye do always resist the Holy Ghost: as your fathers did, so do ye. Which of the prophets have not your fathers persecuted? and they have slain them which shewed before of the coming of the Just One; of whom ye have been now the betrayers and murderers: Who have received the law by the disposition of angels, and have not kept it.
> — Acts 7:51-53

His words "cut to the heart," inflaming them.[10]

> But he, being full of the Holy Ghost, looked up

> stedfastly into heaven, and saw the glory of God, and Jesus standing on the right hand of God, And said, Behold, I see the heavens opened, and the Son of man standing on the right hand of God. —Acts 7:55-56

Enraged, they fell upon him.

> And cast him out of the city, and stoned him: and the witnesses laid down their clothes at a young man's feet, whose name was Saul. And they stoned Stephen, [who was] calling upon God, and saying, Lord Jesus, receive my spirit.
> —Acts 7: 58-59

Stephen's cry was Jesus' cry:

> And when Jesus had cried with a loud voice, he said, Father, into thy hands I commend my spirit: and having said thus, he gave up the ghost. —Luke 23:46

Falling to his knees, Stephen forgave his murderers:

> Lord, lay not this sin to their charge. And when he had said this, he fell asleep. —Acts 7:60

He forgave as Jesus forgave:

> Then said Jesus, Father, forgive them; for they know not what they do. —Luke 23:34

Like Stephen, look "steadfastly into heaven." Look for the One who comes with clouds. Watch to see Jesus, the glory of God.[11]

> But I tell you of a truth, there be some standing here, which shall not taste of death, till they see the kingdom of God. —Luke 9:27

Paul

Paul, who consented in the death of Stephen and stood by as he was stoned (even keeping "the raiment of them that slew him"),[12] became a faithful steward after meeting Jesus on the road to Damascus.

> At midday, O king, I saw in the way a light from heaven, above the brightness of the sun, shining round about me and them which journeyed with me. And when we were all fallen to the earth, I heard a voice speaking unto me, and saying in the Hebrew tongue, Saul, Saul, why persecutest thou me? it is hard for thee to kick against the pricks. And I said, Who art thou, Lord? And he said, I am Jesus whom thou persecutest. But rise, and stand upon thy feet: for I have appeared unto thee for this purpose, to make thee a minister and a witness both of these things which thou hast seen, and of those things in the which I will appear unto thee. —Acts 26:13-16

Soon after, Paul went into Arabia where Jesus revealed the Gospel to him.[13]

> But I certify you, brethren, that the gospel which was preached of me is not after man. For I neither received it of man, neither was I taught it, but by the revelation of Jesus Christ.
> —Galatians 1:11-12

Paul was "in watchings often"[14] and was graced with visions and revelations. The heavens were opened to him, and he was "caught up into paradise."

> I will come to visions and revelations of the Lord. I knew a man in Christ above fourteen years ago, (whether in the body, I cannot tell; or whether out of the body, I cannot tell: God knoweth;) such an one caught up to the third heaven. And I knew such a man, (whether in the body, or out of the body, I cannot tell: God knoweth;) How that he was caught up into paradise, and heard unspeakable words, which it is not lawful for a man to utter.
> —2 Corinthians 12:1-4

Paul had the mind of Christ.[15] He lived in the Spirit and the Spirit empowered him.[c]

> And my speech and my preaching was not with enticing words of man's wisdom, but in demonstration of the Spirit and of power: That your faith should not stand in the wisdom of men, but in the power of God.
> —1 Corinthians 2:4-5

Though he was alive in the Spirit, Paul had not attained "unto the resurrection of the dead." His "vile body" had not yet been changed and "fashioned like unto His [Jesus] glorious body."[16] He was not "already perfect."

---

[c] For though I be absent in the flesh, yet am I with you in the spirit, joying and beholding your order, and the stedfastness of your faith in Christ.
—Colossians 2:5; 1 Corinthians 5:3-5; 2 Kings 5:20-27

The Eye Single

Not as though I had already attained, either were already perfect: but I follow after, if that I may apprehend that for which also I am apprehended of Christ Jesus. Brethren, I count not myself to have apprehended: but this one thing I do, forgetting those things which are behind, and reaching forth unto those things which are before, I press toward the mark for the prize of the high calling of God in Christ Jesus. — Philippians 3:12-14

Celestial Bodies

THE city had no need of the sun, neither of the moon, to shine in it: for the glory of God did lighten it, and the Lamb is the light thereof. —Revelation 21:23

The goal of watching is life in the Spirit. Life in the Spirit requires a spiritual body: "It is sown a natural body; it is raised a spiritual body. There is a natural body, and there is a spiritual body."[1]

> All flesh is not the same flesh: but there is one kind of flesh of men, another flesh of beasts,

> another of fishes, and another of birds. There are also celestial bodies, and bodies terrestrial: but the glory of the celestial is one, and the glory of the terrestrial is another.—1 Corinthians 15:39-40

Celestial bodies are bodies of light. The body of the Man, who appeared to Daniel, "was like the beryl, and his face as the appearance of lightning, and his eyes as lamps of fire."[2] The shepherds of Bethlehem, "keeping watch over their flock by night," were enveloped in the luminous glory of the heralding angel.[3] The angel of the Lord who descended from heaven and rolled back the stone from the door of Jesus' tomb had a "countenance like lightning, and his raiment white as snow."[4] Within the tomb, two men "in shining garments" appeared before the women who had come to anoint the body of our Lord and said to them: "Why seek ye the living among the dead?"[5] When Jesus revealed Himself to John:

> His head and his hairs were white like wool, as white as snow; and his eyes were as a flame of fire; And his feet like unto fine brass, as if they burned in a furnace; and his voice as the sound of many waters. And he had in his right hand seven stars: and out of his mouth went a sharp twoedged sword: and his countenance was as the sun shineth in his strength. And when I saw him, I fell at his feet as dead. And he laid his right hand upon me, saying unto me, Fear not; I am the first and the last: I am he that liveth, and was dead; and, behold, I am alive for evermore, Amen; and have the keys of hell and of death.—Revelation 1:14-18

Because Jesus is light, He could dematerialize in the tomb,

leaving an empty shroud, and re-materialize in the midst of his disciples and say to Thomas, "Reach hither thy finger, and behold my hands; and reach hither thy hand, and thrust it into my side."[6] Jesus could materialize and dematerialize because Light is the substance and power of the universe.[a]

> And he is before all things, and by him all things consist.—Colossians 1:17

God Is Light

> This then is the message which we have heard of him, and declare unto you, that God is light, and in him is no darkness at all.—1 John 1:5

Jesus embodied light.

> I am come a light into the world, that whosoever believeth on me should not abide in darkness. —John 12:46

Light is truth.

> I am the way, the truth, and the life.—John 14:6

Light is life.

> In him was life; and the life was the light of men. —John 1:4

Light is power.

---

[a] That was the true Light, which lighteth every man that cometh into the world. He was in the world, and the world was made by him, and the world knew him not.—John 1:9-10

The Eye Single

> And all the multitude sought to touch him; for power came forth from him, and healed them all. —Luke 6:19 ASV

Light is the radiance of incandescent love.

> For our God is a consuming fire. —Hebrews 12:29

The Clouds Of Heaven

> Hereafter shall ye see the Son of man sitting on the right hand of power, and coming in the clouds of heaven. —Matthew 26:64

Clouds are heavenly bodies; heavenly bodies are spiritual bodies. The Son of man comes in the clouds of heaven, and the clouds that He is in the midst of are our spiritual bodies.

> Behold, he cometh with clouds; and every eye shall see him. —Revelation 1:7

In My Father's House

> IN my Father's house are many mansions: if it were not so, I would have told you. I go to prepare a place for you. And if I go and prepare a place for you, I will come again, and receive you unto myself; that where I am, there ye may be also. —John 14:2-3

When our Father says your mansion is ready, the Son will come for His bride.[a] He will come quickly.[b]

---

[a] But of that day and hour knoweth no man, no, not the angels of heaven, but my Father only.—Matthew 24:36

[b] Behold, I come quickly: hold that fast which thou hast, that no man take thy crown.—Revelation 3:11

> Then shall the kingdom of heaven be likened unto ten virgins, which took their lamps, and went forth to meet the bridegroom. And five of them were wise, and five were foolish. They that were foolish took their lamps, and took no oil with them, but the wise took oil in their vessels with their lamps. While the bridegroom tarried, they all slumbered and slept. And at midnight there was a cry made, Behold, the bridegroom cometh; go ye out to meet him. Then all those virgins arose, and trimmed their lamps. And the foolish said unto the wise, Give us of your oil; for our lamps are gone out. But the wise answered, saying, Not so; lest there be not enough for us and you: but go ye rather to them that sell, and buy for yourselves. And while they went to buy, the bridegroom came; and they that were ready went in with him to the marriage: and the door was shut. Afterward came also the other virgins, saying, Lord, Lord, open to us. But he answered and said, Verily I say unto you, I know you not. Watch therefore, for ye know neither the day nor the hour wherein the Son of man cometh.
> —Matthew 25:1-13

The lamp is the physical body, the vessel is the spiritual body. The oil is the Spirit of God, and the light is the eye single. Jesus is the bridegroom; you are the virgin bride.

> Behold, a virgin shall be with child, and shall bring forth a son, and they shall call his name Emmanuel, which being interpreted is, God with us. —Matthew 1:23

When your celestial home is prepared, Jesus returns. He wakes you with the noise of His coming—a shout and the blast of a trumpet.ᶜ Sleep flees from your eyes as the flame of consciousness burns bright. Charged with power, you rise to meet Him, and union is consummated in the spiritual body He formed while you watched. The Son of man is the celestial body. When you see the Son, you see your mansion.

> And no man hath ascended up to heaven, but he that came down from heaven, even the Son of man which is in heaven.—John 3:13

Before Jesus returns to take you to your heavenly home, there will be signs in the sun, the moon, and stars. There will be effects in consciousness. Because the spiritual body is light, and light is energy, you will experience power as consciousness moves from flesh to spirit.

> There shall be signs in the sun, and in the moon, and in the stars; and upon the earth distress of nations, with perplexity; the sea and the waves roaring; Men's hearts failing them for fear, and for looking after those things which are coming on the earth: for the powers of heaven shall be shaken. And then shall they see the Son of man coming in a cloud with power and great glory. And when these things begin to come to pass, then look up, and lift up your heads; for your redemption draweth nigh.—Luke 21:25-28

Like the wise virgins, let your vessel be full. Watch to exchange the passions of the flesh for the power of the Spirit. Be ready to

---

ᶜ For the Lord himself shall descend from heaven with a shout, with the voice of the archangel, and with the trump of God: and the dead in Christ shall rise first. —1 Thessalonians 4:16

meet Him. Like Jacob, hold onto the Spirit the whole nightlong; do not let go until the day breaks, until you are blessed with the new nature.

> For in this we groan, earnestly desiring to be clothed upon with our house which is from heaven: If so be that being clothed we shall not be found naked. For we that are in this tabernacle do groan, being burdened: not for that we would be unclothed, but clothed upon, that mortality might be swallowed up of life.
> —2 Corinthians 5:2-4

Neither The Day Nor The Hour

But of that day and that hour knoweth no man, no, not the angels which are in heaven, neither the Son, but the Father. Take ye heed, watch and pray: for ye know not when the time is. —Mark 13:32-33

Jesus said:

> Know this, that if the goodman of the house had known in what watch the thief would come, he would have watched, and would not have suffered his house to be broken up. Therefore be ye also ready: for in such an hour as ye think not the Son of man cometh. —Matthew 24:43-44

The Eye Single

Who is this thief that would break in and take what we have?

> Remember therefore how thou hast received and heard, and hold fast, and repent. If therefore thou shalt not watch, I will come on thee as a thief, and thou shalt not know what hour I will come upon thee. — Revelation 3:3

How can our Savior be a thief?

> And he said unto the disciples, The days will come, when ye shall desire to see one of the days of the Son of man, and ye shall not see it. And they shall say to you, See here; or, see there: go not after them, nor follow them. For as the lightning, that lighteneth out of the one part under heaven, shineth unto the other part under heaven; so shall also the Son of man be in his day. But first must he suffer many things, and be rejected of this generation. And as it was in the days of Noe, so shall it be also in the days of the Son of man. They did eat, they drank, they married wives, they were given in marriage, until the day that Noe entered into the ark, and the flood came, and destroyed them all. Likewise also as it was in the days of Lot; they did eat, they drank, they bought, they sold, they planted, they builded; But the same day that Lot went out of Sodom it rained fire and brimstone from heaven, and destroyed them all. Even thus shall it be in the day when the Son of man is revealed. In that day, he which shall be upon the housetop, and his stuff in the house, let him not come down to take it away: and he that is in the field, let him likewise not return back. Remember Lot's wife. Whosoever

> shall seek to save his life shall lose it; and whosoever shall lose his life shall preserve it. I tell you, in that night there shall be two men in one bed; the one shall be taken, and the other shall be left. Two women shall be grinding together; the one shall be taken, and the other left. Two men shall be in the field; the one shall be taken, and the other left. —Luke 17:22-36

There are two bodies (flesh and spirit) but only one soul, one consciousness. Jesus comes for the spirit man; the carcass is left behind.[a]

> And they answered and said unto him, Where, Lord? And he said unto them, Wheresoever the body is, thither will the eagles be gathered together. —Luke 17:37

If you are watching when Jesus returns for you in spirit, you see Him and ascend with Him in spirit. If you are not watching, your house is "broken up," and you . . . cut "in sunder."

Be ready to wake and watch. Do not let the thief break in and steal; do not let him take your spiritual substance. Watch to be in the Spirit. Watch, and you "shall mount up with wings as eagles."[b] Whatever you are doing that day, stop. Look to see Jesus. Watch! "Whosoever shall seek to save his life shall lose it; and whosoever shall lose his life shall preserve it."

Watch! This is "the day when the Son of man is revealed." "For as the lightning, that lighteneth out of the one part under heaven,

---

[a] For wheresoever the carcase is, there will the eagles be gathered together. —Matthew 24:28

[b] But they that wait upon the LORD shall renew their strength; they shall mount up with wings as eagles; they shall run, and not be weary; and they shall walk, and not faint. —Isaiah 40:31

shineth unto the other part under heaven; so shall also the Son of man be in his day." Enter the ark; leave Sodom behind.

But if you miss the moment, if you go back rather than forward, if you do not leave everyone and everything and go to meet Him, you are left in the flesh. All that you watched and waited for is taken from you: the love, the joy, the peace and power. "There shall be weeping and gnashing of teeth" when you realize how close you came and how much you lost.[1]

> And if that servant say in his heart, My Lord delayeth his coming; and shall begin to beat the menservants and maidens, and to eat and drink, and to be drunken; The Lord of that servant will come in a day when he looketh not for him, and at an hour when he is not aware, and will cut him in sunder, and will appoint him his portion with the unbelievers. — Luke 12:45-46

You will be like Samson with his hair cut off and his eyes put out. Chained and imprisoned in your body of flesh, the only way out will be back to the grindstone.[2] Back to watching and waiting, blind to the world, watching for the power of God to return. Waiting for another chance to bring down the Philistine temple.[3]

Watch, therefore. Feast on Jesus. Give flesh to your body of light.

> For ye were sometimes darkness, but now are ye light in the Lord: walk as children of light.
> —Ephesians 5:8

Commanding Faith

*T*HEN said they unto him, What shall we do, that we might work the works of God? Jesus answered and said unto them, This is the work of God, that ye believe on him whom he hath sent. —John 6:28-29

Jesus gave a parable about the efficacy of humble, yet bold and persistent, prayer.

> There was in a city a judge, which feared not God, neither regarded man: And there was a widow in that city; and she came unto him, saying, Avenge me of mine adversary. And he would not for a while: but afterward he said within

> himself, Though I fear not God, nor regard man; Yet because this widow troubleth me, I will avenge her, lest by her continual coming she weary me. And the Lord said, Hear what the unjust judge saith. And shall not God avenge his own elect, which cry day and night unto him, though he bear long with them? I tell you that he will avenge them speedily. —Luke 18:1-8

The unjust judge "feared not God, neither regarded man." The widow's problems were nothing to Him; they were "time and chance" that "happeneth" to all. He was concerned for his own sake and his own sake alone:

> For mine own sake, even for mine own sake, will I do it: for how should my name be polluted? and I will not give my glory unto another.
> —Isaiah 48:11

What was good for the importunate widow was good for the unjust judge.

> For the LORD'S portion is his people; Jacob is the lot of his inheritance. —Deuteronomy 32:9

God is the unjust judge.

> I returned, and saw under the sun, that the race is not to the swift, nor the battle to the strong, neither yet bread to the wise, nor yet riches to men of understanding, nor yet favour to men of skill; but time and chance happeneth to them all. —Ecclesiastes 9:11

The widow is the church.

> Wives, submit yourselves unto your own husbands, as unto the Lord. For the husband is the head of the wife, even as Christ is the head of the church: and he is the saviour of the body.
> —Ephesians 5:22-23

Life is often unfair and unjust. Not everyone is born well off, and bad things happen to good people. When things go wrong, we cry out. We pray, but often . . . no answer. We wait and, at times, no help comes. Some say no is an answer and stop praying, stop waiting, but not the widow.

In the Spirit of her crucified husband, the widow has faith that the Unjust Judge will do her good and not evil, faith that He will answer prayer, faith that He will avenge her upon her adversary. She is always present—watching, waiting, asking. She hangs on and does not let go. So should we.

> But without faith it is impossible to please him: for he that cometh to God must believe that he is, and that he is a rewarder of them that diligently seek him.—Hebrews 11:6

Have faith of God.[1] "Troubleth" the Unjust Judge. When you trouble Him, you trouble yourself. Demand it of yourself.

> And the apostles said unto the Lord, Increase our faith. And the Lord said, If ye had faith as a grain of mustard seed, ye might say unto this sycamine tree, Be thou plucked up by the root, and be thou planted in the sea; and it should obey you.—Luke 17:5-6

Faith On The Earth

> Nevertheless when the Son of man cometh, shall he find faith on the earth?—Luke 18:8

The Eye Single

That's up to you. Do you give Him no rest? Do you cry out night and day? Jesus made it clear, "The kingdom of God is within you."[2]

> Foxes have holes, and the birds of the air have nests; but the Son of man hath not where to lay his head. —Matthew 8:20

Look into Being, look until you see the Son of man coming in the clouds of heaven. Fathom the God of love, who gives all when He gives Himself. Cast out demon pride whose last refuge is the sainted sinner. Embrace Jesus "that ye might be filled with all the fulness of God."[3] Cast off false humility, for "except ye be converted, and become as little children, ye shall not enter into the kingdom of heaven."[4] No longer a sainted sinner, look expectantly at God your Father. Like children, who love Christmas best of all, glory in the love of your Father, who glories in giving all. Glory in His love.

> He that spared not his own Son, but delivered him up for us all, how shall he not with him also freely give us all things? —Romans 8:32

Who Is This Son Of Man?

> The people answered him, We have heard out of the law that Christ abideth for ever: and how sayest thou, The Son of man must be lifted up? Who is this Son of man? Then Jesus said unto them, Yet a little while is the light with you. Walk while ye have the light, lest darkness come upon you: for he that walketh in darkness knoweth not whither he goeth.
> —John 12:34-35

"Who is this Son of man?"

He is Jesus, the son of the heavenly Man, the only begotten Son of God, son of Mary. He is Jesus, son of the earthly man who gives birth to Him in the stable of his flesh. The Son of man is "Christ in you, the hope of glory."[5]

> In whom are hid all the treasures of wisdom and knowledge. —Colossians 2:3

Jesus said, *"Let these sayings sink down into your ears: for the Son of man shall be delivered into the hands of men."*[6] The Son of man was delivered into the hands of men in the Garden of Gethsemane. He is ours to do with as we will. Those who will to receive light are children of Light. Those who will not, Jesus "departed and did hide himself from them."[7]

The Son of man is "Alpha and Omega, the beginning and the end, the first and the last."[8] His birth in us is the goal of life. In Him, God will be all in all.

> When all things shall be subdued unto him, then shall the Son also himself be subject unto him that put all things under him, that God may be all in all. —1 Corinthians 15:28

Alive!
I know
With eye single,
Not shadow,
Light,
Grace descending
Putting out night.
One mind,
One Spirit,
Alpha and Omega
Completing
Beginning.

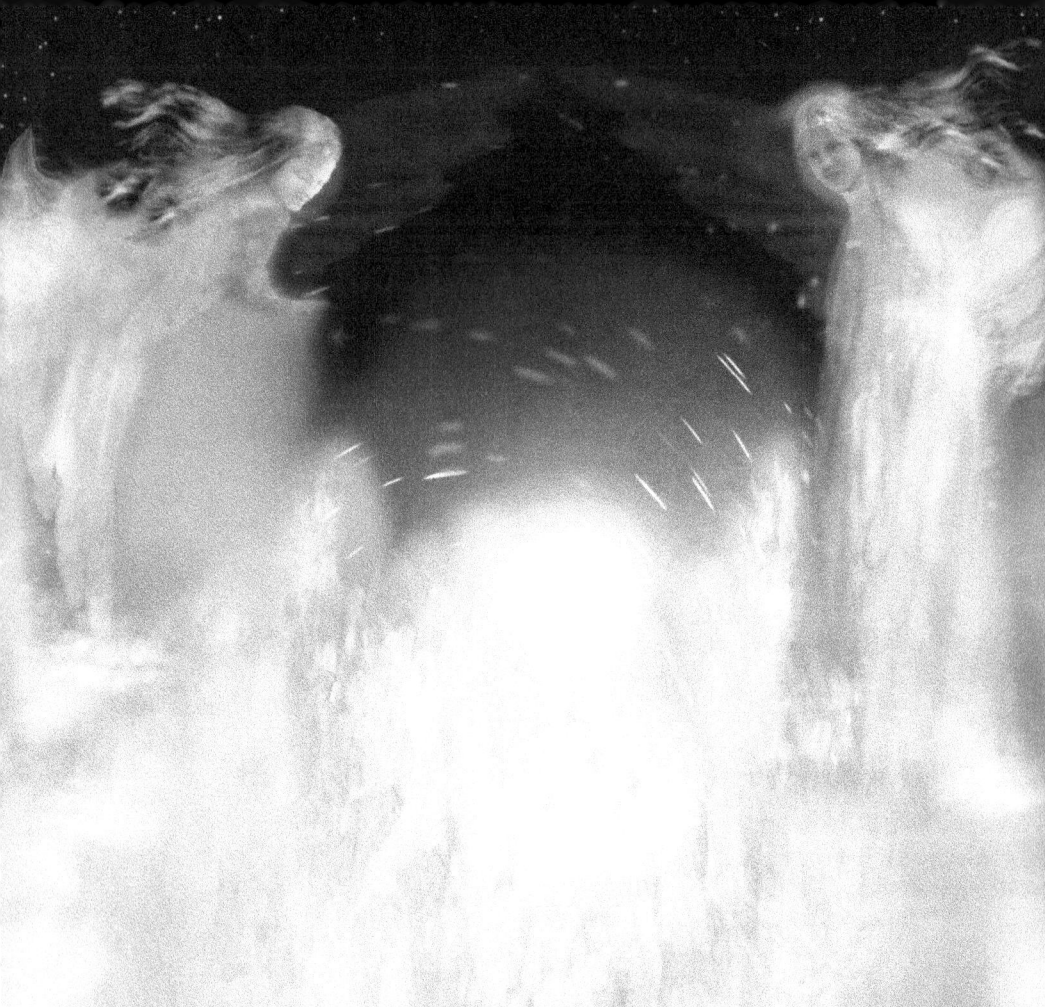

*N*ow we have received,
not the spirit of the world,
but the spirit which is of God;
that we might know the things
that are freely given to us of God.

1 Corinthians 2:12

SEEING INTO HEAVEN

Heavenly Things
Son Of Perdition
The Struggle With Sleep
Living In The Spirit
When The Trumpet Sounds Long
The Prayer

Heavenly Things

*O*NE thing have I desired of the LORD, that will I seek after; that I may dwell in the house of the LORD all the days of my life, to behold the beauty of the LORD, and to enquire in his temple. — Psalms 27:4

Watching is a fast for the soul; watching is a feast. Watching is *seeing* God.

> We speak that we do know, and testify that we have seen; and ye receive not our witness. If I have told you earthly things, and ye believe not, how shall ye believe, if I tell you of heavenly things? — John 3:11-12

Watching is as natural as breathing. We do it all the time. It is how we know. We open our physical senses and take the world in. We see, hear, feel, smell, taste, and know by knowing nothing. Then we process with our minds what we have sensed with our bodies. When we watch for Jesus, we open our spiritual senses to watch with Him. We see Him, we feel Him, we know Him—our spirits assimilate Him.

> For now we see through a glass, darkly; but then face to face: now I know in part; but then shall I know even as also I am known.
> —1 Corinthians 13:12

Watching frees from the flesh for life in the Spirit. Once you are free, remain free. Let the life and power of the Spirit build in you. Watch and wait. Wait, watch.

> Blessed is the man that heareth me, watching daily at my gates, waiting at the posts of my doors.
> —Proverbs 8:34

> I will stand upon my watch, and set me upon the tower, and will watch to see what he will say unto me, and what I shall answer when I am reproved.—Habakkuk 2:1

> I am like a pelican of the wilderness: I am like an owl of the desert. I watch, and am as a sparrow alone upon the house top.—Psalms 102:6-7

When To Watch

Watch always: watch in the quiet of the night, watch in the hush of the morning, watch throughout the day. Be alert and attentive. Watch as for a friend who will arrive at any moment.

> "Go, set a watchman," the LORD told Isaiah. "Let him declare what he seeth." And the watchman said, "My lord, I stand continually upon the watchtower in the daytime, and I am set in my ward whole nights." —Isaiah 21:6-8

The best time for watching is early morning when you are fresh from sleep and not yet entangled in the concerns of the day.

> In the morning will I order my prayer unto thee, and will keep watch. —Psalms 5:3 ASV

Jesus may wake you, as He did Samuel. He may call your name, for "he calleth his own sheep by name and leadeth them out."[1]

> And the LORD came and stood, and called as at other times, *"Samuel, Samuel."* Then Samuel answered, *"Speak; for thy servant heareth."*
> —1 Samuel 3:10

You might hear a knock, a doorbell, or a phone ringing. No matter how you are awakened, say yes. Rise up quickly and watch. When you do, the spiritual energy that wakes you vivifies you.

> As for me, I will behold thy face in righteousness: I shall be satisfied, when I awake, with thy likeness.
> —Psalms 17:15

Jesus rose early to pray. He was "up a great while before day, he went out, and departed into a solitary place, and there prayed."[2] He rose to pray and watch with the Father:

> Verily, verily, I say unto you, The Son can do

> nothing of himself, but what he seeth the Father do: for what things soever he doeth, these also doeth the Son likewise. —John 5:19

> I speak that which I have seen with my Father. —John 8:38

Watch every day. Do not miss a day lest you lose what you have gained. Each day, gather the manna, fill your vessel, feed your spirit man. Do not let him die for lack of Bread. "God is a spirit." To starve your spirit man is to put God to death in you— is to kill God. If you kill God, God will kill you! He will take back His Spirit, killing your spirit man.

> It is the Spirit that quickeneth; the flesh profiteth nothing: the words that I speak unto you, they are spirit, and they are life. —John 6:63

Let God live. Watch with Jesus. Let Him change you into Himself. It is pure grace.

> But the hour cometh, and now is, when the true worshippers shall worship the Father in spirit and in truth: for the Father seeketh such to worship him. God is a Spirit: and they that worship him must worship him in spirit and in truth. —John 4:23-24

Every watch charges your body with spiritual power. With every watch, power builds. Eventually, you will hear and feel the power of the Spirit move within you at different times throughout the day and night. When you do, it is a call to watch. Listen to the sound, feel the essence, embrace the Spirit. Let the Spirit embrace you. Enter His presence, the presence of Another. Sit with Him,

The Eye Single

gaze upon Him, spend time with your Lover—the One you love.

> The wind bloweth where it listeth, and thou hearest the sound thereof, but canst not tell whence it cometh, and whither it goeth: so is every one that is born of the Spirit.—John 3:8

How To Watch

Look for Jesus when you watch. Those who *see* Jesus are one with Jesus: "He that is joined unto the Lord is one spirit."[3] Look to see Him and your consciousness is focused, contained and enhanced. Your spirit comes alive.

> I wait for the LORD, my soul doth wait, and in his word do I hope. My soul waiteth for the LORD more than they that watch for the morning: I say, more than they that watch for the morning.—Psalms 130:5-6

If you are not mindful of Him, your consciousness flows into your surroundings, wanders into fantasy, or slips into sleep. Your spirit remains unaffected, and your watching … fruitless.

> Unless the LORD builds the house, those who build it labor in vain. Unless the LORD watches over the city, the watchman stays awake in vain.—Psalms 127:1 ESV

As you quiet yourself at the start of a watch, pressing concerns may come to mind. Give them the attention they demand. Have pen and paper at hand, jot notes to yourself. Then be still.

> My soul, wait thou in silence for God only; For my expectation is from him.—Psalms 62:5

Rest your eyes on whatever is comfortable: the sky, the horizon, or a treetop a mile away; a cross, a corner, or an empty glass across the room—waiting to be filled. In the night, embrace the darkness, for "the darkness is past, and the true light now shineth."[4] Gaze upon the heavens. He waits to fill you.

> And there shall be no night there; and they need no candle, neither light of the sun; for the Lord God giveth them light: and they shall reign for ever and ever.—Revelation 22:5

Become one with the light of life. Live in the light.

> For with thee is the fountain of life: in thy light shall we see light.—Psalms 36:9

Watch And Pray

> Watch ye therefore, and pray always, that ye may be accounted worthy to escape all these things that shall come to pass, and to stand before the Son of man.—Luke 21:36

Prayer and watching are complementary. They are two sides of the same coin: one is talking, the other listening; one is asking, the other receiving; one is seeking, the other seeing. To watch and pray is to "pray without ceasing,"[5] yet without vain repetition.[6]

Ways To Pray While Watching

Simply watch, and the Spirit intercedes for you.

> Likewise the Spirit also helpeth our infirmities: for we know not what we should pray for as

> we ought: but the Spirit itself maketh intercession for us with groanings which cannot be uttered. And he that searcheth the hearts knoweth what is the mind of the Spirit, because he maketh intercession for the saints according to the will of God. —Romans 8:26-27

Pray what is on your heart, as Jesus did at Gethsemane.[7]

> Continue in prayer, and watch in the same with thanksgiving. —Colossians 4:2

Pray with the spirit.[a]

> But ye, beloved, building up yourselves on your most holy faith, praying in the Holy Ghost, Keep yourselves in the love of God, looking for the mercy of our Lord Jesus Christ unto eternal life. —Jude 1:20-21

Pray the prayer of praise.

> Praise ye the LORD. Praise the LORD, O my soul. —Psalms 146:1

Watch and pray Jesus' prayer:

> After this manner therefore pray ye: Our Father which art in heaven, Hallowed be thy name. Thy kingdom come. Thy will be done in earth, as it is in heaven. Give us this day our daily bread. And forgive us our debts, as we forgive our debtors. And lead us not into

---

[a] He that speaketh in an unknown tongue edifieth himself. —1 Corinthians 14:4

> temptation, but deliver us from evil: For thine is the kingdom, and the power, and the glory, for ever. Amen. — Matthew 6:9-13

Just pray.

> Pray without ceasing. In every thing give thanks: for this is the will of God in Christ Jesus concerning you. — 1 Thessalonians 5:17-18

Son Of Perdition

> THE light of the body is the eye: there-fore when thine eye is single, thy whole body also is full of light; but when thine eye is evil, thy body also is full of darkness. Take heed therefore that the light which is in thee be not darkness.
> —Luke 11:34-35

Beware "the evil one."

> We know that whosoever is begotten of God sinneth not; but he that was begotten of God keepeth himself, and the evil one toucheth him not. —1 John 5:18 ASV

He will resist watching in every way and try to substitute himself for the life of Jesus.

> Let no man deceive you by any means: for that day shall not come, except there come a falling away first, and that man of sin be revealed, the son of perdition; Who opposeth and exalteth himself above all that is called God, or that is worshipped; so that he as God sitteth in the temple of God, shewing himself that he is God.
> —2 Thessalonians 2:3-4

The son of perdition will distract you with fantasy and tempt you with sleep. He lives in dark light and resides in the flesh as the man of sin but is held in check by the Spirit. He would diffuse the light into unfocused, uncontrolled energies; for the light of the eye single exposes him, and he is destroyed by the brightness of Jesus' coming. Light extinguishes darkness; watching casts out the evil one.

> Remember ye not, that, when I was yet with you, I told you these things? And now ye know what withholdeth that he might be revealed in his time. For the mystery of iniquity doth already work: only he who now letteth will let, until he be taken out of the way. And then shall that Wicked be revealed, whom the Lord shall consume with the spirit of his mouth, and shall destroy with the brightness of his coming: Even him, whose coming is after the working of Satan with all power and signs and lying wonders, And with all deceivableness of unrighteousness in them that perish; because they received not the love of the truth, that they might be saved.
> —2 Thessalonians 2:5-10

The Eye Single

When the man of sin makes you sleepy, refresh yourself. Get up and walk around, pour a cup of coffee, and watch again. If he distracts you, call on Jesus: "Jesus, Jesus, come Lord Jesus." Jesus' name is above all names; it is the name by which we are saved. He wants us to be conscious in His Spirit. He wants us to *see* Him.

> Humble yourselves in the sight of the Lord, and he shall lift you up. —James 4:10

The Struggle With Sleep

YE are all the children of light, and the children of the day: we are not of the night, nor of darkness. Therefore let us not sleep, as do others; but let us watch and be sober.
—1 Thessalonians 5:5-6

As you continue to watch daily, you will sleep less and watch more. Yet sleep will always be tempting, always tagging along, always waiting for an opportunity to feed on the energies of life.[a] Its momentary pleasure is intensified by the increased life force.

---

[a] And when the devil had ended all the temptation, he departed from him for a season.—Luke 4:13

The Eye Single

Do not be seduced by sleep's allure. Sleep will sap your spirit and leave you enervated. Falling asleep after watching is like turning your car engine off while leaving the headlights on. By morning, your soul will be drained of all power.

Still, if you choose to sleep, refocus your consciousness. Move your mind from spirit back to flesh by attending to a temporal subject or activity. Give your body time to ground and absorb the energies of the Spirit. Otherwise, the power that quickens wastes in the flesh: the manna breeds worms and stinks.[1] What is born in watching dies in sleep.

As you near the breakthrough into the Spirit of Jesus, the need for sleep decreases as the power of the Spirit increases. Rise when the Spirit wakes you, rise up and enter in—and shut the door behind you![b] Do not remain in the twilight. Do not let the evil one—the man of sin[c]—assault you in oppressive dreams and visions. He has many disguises, many forms and faces. He comes to take all for which you have watched and waited, to destroy all that you have gained. He comes to steal your life and kill your spirit man. Husband your life. Rise and watch.

> The thief cometh not, but for to steal, and to kill, and to destroy: I am come that they might have life, and that they might have it more abundantly.
> —John 10:10

Just before His crucifixion, Jesus left Jerusalem nightly to go to the Garden of Gethsemane to watch and pray.[2] He was at the end

---

[b] But thou, when thou prayest, enter into thy closet, and when thou hast shut thy door, pray to thy Father which is in secret; and thy Father which seeth in secret shall reward thee openly.—Matthew 6:6

[c] For I know that in me (that is, in my flesh,) dwelleth no good thing: for to will is present with me; but how to perform that which is good I find not. For the good that I would I do not: but the evil which I would not, that I do. Now if I do that I would not, it is no more I that do it, but sin that dwelleth in me.—Romans 7:18-20

of His earthly ministry and said to His disciples, "*I have overcome the world.*"³ Did He who had overcome the world rest in sleep, or did He rest in God?

On the night that He was betrayed, Jesus brought His disciples with Him to the Garden of Gethsemane. He said, "*Sit ye here, while I go and pray yonder.*" Then He took with Him Peter, James and John, and said to them, "*My soul is exceeding sorrowful, even unto death: tarry ye here, and watch with me.*"⁴

But they slept. They slept "for sorrow."ᵈ Jesus woke them. A little while later, He woke them again—to no avail.

> And he cometh, and findeth them sleeping, and saith unto Peter, Simon, sleepest thou? Couldest not thou watch one hour? Watch ye and pray, lest ye enter into temptation. The spirit truly is ready, but the flesh is weak. And again he went away, and prayed, and spake the same words. And when he returned, he found them asleep again, (for their eyes were heavy), neither wist they what to answer him. And he cometh the third time, and saith unto them, Sleep on now, and take your rest: it is enough, the hour is come; behold, the Son of man is betrayed into the hands of sinners.—Mark 14:37-41

When Jesus was arrested, the disciples "scattered."⁵ The disciples, for their own sakes, should have watched with Jesus. If they had, they would have resisted temptation. They would have stood with Him.

> Watch ye, stand fast in the faith, quit you like men, be strong.—1 Corinthians 16:13

ᵈ And when he rose from prayer, and was come to his disciples, he found them sleeping for sorrow.—Luke 22:45

The Eye Single

Sleep should not be a longed for refuge.

> Why sleep ye? rise and pray, lest ye enter into temptation. —Luke 22:46

Replace it with the "armour of light."

> It is high time to awake out of sleep: for now is our salvation nearer than when we believed. The night is far spent, the day is at hand: let us therefore cast off the works of darkness, and let us put on the armour of light. —Romans 13:11-12

Watch with Jesus. Enter into the joy of the Lord.

> And now come I to thee; and these things I speak in the world, that they might have my joy fulfilled in themselves. —John 17:13

Living In The Spirit

The disciple is not above his master: but every one that is perfect shall be as his master.
—Luke 6:40

The purpose of watching is the transfer of consciousness from flesh to spirit: life in the Spirit of Jesus while still in the body.

> But if the Spirit of him that raised up Jesus from the dead dwell in you, he that raised up Christ from the dead shall also quicken your mortal bodies by his Spirit that dwelleth in you.
> —Romans 8:11

Those who live in the Spirit never die.

> I am the resurrection, and the life: he that believeth in me, though he were dead, yet shall he live: And whosoever liveth and believeth in me shall never die. —John 11:25-26

Death is birth, a crossing to glory. Death is "swallowed up of life."

> For we know that if our earthly house of this tabernacle were dissolved, we have a building of God, an house not made with hands, eternal in the heavens. For in this we groan, earnestly desiring to be clothed upon with our house which is from heaven: If so be that being clothed we shall not be found naked. For we that are in this tabernacle do groan, being burdened: not for that we would be unclothed, but clothed upon, that mortality might be swallowed up of life. —2 Corinthians 5:1-4

When we see the Son of man coming in the clouds of heaven, "we shall all be changed, in a moment, in the twinkling of an eye."[1] Like lightning, we will be "clothed upon with our house which is from heaven." Now, we are in Jesus and He is in us. Then, we receive our adoption and awake in the Spirit. Now, we have power to become the sons of God.[2] Then, we are the sons of God.

> And he said unto me, It is done. I am Alpha and Omega, the beginning and the end. I will give unto him that is athirst of the fountain of the water of life freely. He that overcometh shall inherit all things; and I will be his God, and he shall be my son. —Revelation 21:6-7

When The Trumpet Sounds Long

WATCH for Jesus' return; His return is our hope. We will receive our adoption; we will be changed into His image. We will be as He is and as He was—alive in both the spirit and the flesh.

> For we are saved by hope: but hope that is seen is not hope: for what a man seeth, why doth he yet hope for? But if we hope for that we see not, then do we with patience wait for it.
> —Romans 8:24-25

Watch for Jesus with all your heart, all your soul, all your mind, and all your strength.

> And thou shalt love the Lord thy God with all thy heart, and with all thy soul, and with all thy mind, and with all thy strength: this is the first commandment. —Mark 12:30

Be violent about it.

> The law and the prophets were until John: from that time the gospel of the kingdom of God is preached, and every man entereth violently into it. —Luke 16:16 ASV

Die to the world.

> Whosoever doth not bear his cross, and come after me, cannot be my disciple. —Luke 14:27

Friendship with the world is enmity with God.

> Ye adulterers and adulteresses, know ye not that the friendship of the world is enmity with God? whosoever therefore will be a friend of the world is the enemy of God. —James 4:4

Hate your own life.

> If any man come to me, and hate not his father, and mother, and wife, and children, and brethren, and sisters, yea, and his own life also, he cannot be my disciple. —Luke 14:26

Forsake all that you have.

> Likewise, whosoever he be of you that forsaketh not all that he hath, he cannot be my disciple.
> —Luke 14:33

Will you forsake everyone and everything for the love of Jesus? Pray with your whole heart, "Lord Jesus, come!" Then watch whenever you can for as long as you can. Prepare for watching like a runner prepares for a race. Be temperate in all things, and do not let the world weigh upon you; do not let it make you physically or mentally fatigued. Save your life for Jesus.

> Know ye not that they which run in a race run all, but one receiveth the prize? So run, that ye may obtain. And every man that striveth for the mastery is temperate in all things. Now they do it to obtain a corruptible crown; but we an incorruptible. —1 Corinthians 9:24-25

On the day the trumpet sounds long and the power of God is upon you, leave all to watch for Jesus.[a] Do not go back for anyone or anything.

> For the Lord himself shall descend from heaven with a shout, with the voice of the archangel, and with the trump of God: and the dead in Christ shall rise first: Then we which are alive and remain shall be caught up together with them in the clouds, to meet the Lord in the air: and so shall we ever be with the Lord. —1 Thessalonians 4:16-17

> But the day of the Lord will come as a thief in the night; in the which the heavens shall pass away with a great noise, and the elements shall melt with fervent heat, the earth also and the works that are therein shall be burned up.
> —2 Peter 3:10

---

[a] When the trumpet soundeth long, they shall come up to the mount. —Exodus 19:13

Then shall appear the sign of the Son of man in heaven: and then shall all the tribes of the earth mourn, and they shall see the Son of man coming in the clouds of heaven with power and great glory. — Matthew 24:30

"Come, Lord Jesus."

The grace of our Lord Jesus Christ be with you all. Amen. — Revelation 22:20-21

The Prayer

Father

Make my will the same as your will

I want to do your will

Fill me with desire for what you want

Fill me with your being

Notes

PAGE iv

1. Eckhart von Hochheim (Meister Eckhart), *Sermon 1V: True Hearing*, (c. 14th century). Retrieved from www.ccel.org
2. William Blake, "Auguries of Innocence," *The Penguin Book of English Verse*, ed. John Hayward, London: Book Club Associates, 1978.

PAGE viii

1. Robert Jamieson, A. R. Fausset and David Brown, 1 John 3:2, in *A Commentary, Critical and Explanatory, on the Old and New Testaments*, vol. 2, Hartford, Conn: S.S. Scranton & Co., 1876, p.531.
Retrieved from http://catalog.hathitrust.org/Record/008729238
2. Irenaeus, *Adversus Haereses* (c. 180), 20:7, book 4, in *Five Books of S. Irenaeus, Bishop of Lyons, Against Heresies*, trans. John Keble, Oxford: James Parker, 1872, p.369.
Retrieved from http://archive.org/details/fivebooksofsiren42iren

IINTRODUCTION
1. 2 Peter 3:12
2. Titus 2:13
3. Isaiah 2:5

AWAKE

WATCH
1. Mark 13:37
2. Revelation 22:20
3. John 1:51
4. Acts 7:56
5. Matthew 24:27
6. John 21:22
7. Acts 9:10-17
8. Galatians 1:11-12
9. Acts 26:15-16
10. Acts 1:6-9; Luke 19:11-27

NOTES

11. John 4:19-24
12. Luke 17:5-10
13. Psalms 65:1 LITV
14. Romans 10:13
15. Philippians 2:9
16. Acts 4:12

A New Beginning
1. Which was the son of Enos, which was the son of Seth, which was the son of Adam, which was the son of God.—Luke 3:38
2. Genesis 2:7
3. Matthew 25:34-40
4. 1 Corinthians 15:45-49
5. And Adam called his wife's name Eve; because she was the mother of all living.—Genesis 3:20

The Truth Of Faith
1. Numbers 14:14 YLT; 2 Corinthians 3:18
2. The apple of the eye is the pupil of the eye. John McClintock and James Strong, *Cyclopædia of Biblical, Theological and Ecclesiastical Literature*, vol. 1, New York: Harper & Bros., 1895, p.325. Retrieved from https://babel.hathitrust.org/cgi/pt?id=uva.x001645428;view=2up;seq=4

FROM DARKNESS TO LIGHT

The Almond Tree
1. Genesis 27:41-46, 28:1-4
2. Mark 12:10
3. William Smith, ed., *A Dictionary of the Bible: Comprising Its Antiquities, Biography, Geography, and Natural History*, In Three Volumes, London: John Murray, 1863, vol. 1, p.198.
   Retrieved from https://catalog.hathitrust.org/Record/007911777
4. John McClintock and James Strong, vol. 5 (1894), p.582. Retrieved from https://babel.hathitrust.org/cgi/pt?id=uva.x001645332;view=2up;seq=4
5. Exodus 25:31-40. The golden lampstand in the Holy Place of the Tabernacle was in the form of a stylized almond tree.
6. Adam Clarke, *The Holy Bible, containing the Old and New Testaments: Authorised translations, including the Marginal Readings and Parallel Texts, with a Commentary and Critical Notes*, vol. 4, New York: G. Lane & P. P. Sandford, 1843, p.256.
   Retrieved from https://archive.org/details/holybiblecontain184604clar

7. And God said unto Moses, I AM THAT I AM.—Exodus 3:14. Literally, '*I will be what I will be.*' Clarke, vol. 1, p.304. Retrieved from https://archive.org/details/holybiblecontai01clar
8. John 10:30

WRESTLING GOD
1. Genesis 27:41
2. Genesis 32:6-12
3. Genesis 3:8; 18:1-33
4. Smith, vol. 1, p.912.
5. Genesis 25:26
6. And he said, Is not he rightly named Jacob? for he hath supplanted me these two times: he took away my birthright; and, behold, now he hath taken away my blessing.—Genesis 27:36. Also Genesis 25:21-26
7. Genesis 32:9
8. 1 Timothy 6:17
9. Psalms 127:2 ASV
10. Genesis 27:35
11. Genesis 33:10
12. Exodus 3:14-15
13. Acts 17:28

ABRAHAM'S SEED
1. Genesis 1:26-28; Genesis 22:16-18; Genesis 26:3-5. The birthright belonged to the firstborn, but could be lost due to sin (Genesis 4:7; 1 Chronicles 5:1). Given with the blessing, the birthright conferred power and authority (Genesis 27:29; Genesis 27:37). In addition to the general inheritance, the holder of the birthright received a double portion of the father's property (Deuteronomy 21:17).
2. Genesis 25:28-34
3. Genesis 2:16-17
4. Romans 9:13
5. Hosea 12:4 LITV
6. Mark 14:34
7. Gethsemane means *oil press* in Aramaic. *New Bible Dictionary Second Edition*, Wheaton, Il: Tyndale, reprint 1987.
8. Exodus 4:22; Jeremiah 31:9
9. John 1:1-3,14
10. Colossians 1:12-20
11. Ephesians 2:8

NOTES

12. Hebrews 5:7
13. Matthew 26:38
14. Hebrews 7:25
15. Romans 8:26

Consuming The Flesh
1. Psalms 105:17; Philippians 2:5-9
2. Genesis 37:24-28
3. Genesis 39:22
4. 1 Peter 3:18-20; Matthew 12:38-41; Psalms 16:8-11
5. 1 Corinthians 15:24-28
6. Exodus 13:19
7. Exodus 1:8-14
8. Matthew 2:14-15
9. Exodus 12:3
10. Luke 9:23
11. 1 Corinthians 11:24
12. 1 Corinthians 11:31
13. Exodus 19:4

Cloud And Fire
1. 2 Thessalonians 2:3-4
2. Zephaniah 3:15
3. Exodus 3:14

Bread From Heaven
1. 1 Corinthians 2:7-8
2. Luke 18:7
3. John 14:9
4. Ephesians 5:14

Mount Sinai
1. Hebrews 12:14
2. 1 Thessalonians 4:17
3. 1 Corinthians 15:52
4. Acts 6:15
5. Exodus 19:19
6. 2 Timothy 4:8

Built By God
1. *New Bible Dictionary Second Edition.*
2. 2 Corinthians 5:1
3. Exodus 33:7

4. Acts 6:15
5. Colossians 1:15
6. Exodus 33:11
7. Jesus is the Greek form of the Hebrew *Joshua*. Smith, vol. 1, p.1143. Retrieved from https://catalog.hathitrust.org/Record/007911777
8. Ephesians 4:24

The Tabernacle And Cherubim
1. Exodus 25:8
2. The first Tabernacle of the Congregation was Moses' personal tent. Exodus 18:13-16; 33:7
3. Exodus 26:1; 26:31
4. John 15:5
5. Ezekiel 41:25
6. Revelation 5:5; 22:14
7. Ezekiel 1:1
8. Ezekiel 1:20

I Am
1. Job 12:10
2. Psalms 106:23
3. Hebrews 3:5
4. Hebrews 1:3

God As Self
1. Exodus 24:18; Exodus 34:28; Deuteronomy 9:9
2. Luke 11:20

The Fiery Serpent
1. John 3:14
2. Genesis 3:6
3. Mark 15:25; Luke 23:44-46

Standing Still In Jordan
1. Revelation 5:9-10; Matthew 26:27-28
2. Smith, vol. 1, p.1126.
3. Matthew 3:16
4. 1 Thessalonians 4:17
5. 2 Corinthians 5:17

Empty Vessels
1. Judges 7:2-3
2. Judges 7:7
3. Judges 8:10

NOTES

4. Job 33:14-18
5. Matthew 26:40-41
6. 1 Corinthians 15:26

THE DOUBLE PORTION
1. 2 Kings 1:8; Matthew 3:4
2. 1 Kings 17:24
3. 1 Kings 17:16-24
4. 2 Kings 1:10
5. 1 Kings 18:41-45
6. Exodus 33:18-23
7. 1 King 19:9
8. 1 Corinthians 3:16

FIRST ELIJAH, THEN ELISHA
1. 1 Kings 19:16
2. Luke 10:17-18
3. 1 Thessalonians 4:17
4. 2 Kings 2:9-10
5. John 6:62

I KNOW MY REDEEMER LIVETH
1. Job 42:7-8
2. Job 12:10
3. Acts 17:28
4. Exodus 33:22-23
5. Job 42:12

COMES MY BELOVED
1. Song of Solomon 2:1
2. Revelation 22:20

THE BRIGHT AND MORNING STAR

THE MESSENGER
1. Luke 1:36
2. Matthew 3:11; Matthew 11:3
3. Luke 3:2
4. John 5:35
5. Luke 3:3
6. Matthew 3:2
7. Luke 3:8
8. Luke 3:10-14

9. Matthew 5:20
10. Mark 6:17-18; Luke: 3:19-20
11. Mark 6:19-20

THE WATCHMAN
1. Various etymologies of 'Nazareth' have been proposed. The idea that it means *'consecrated,' 'devoted to God'* (from נָדַר, whence Nazirite), or that it denotes *'my Saviour'* (נוֹצְרִי), may be dismissed at once. Equally improbable is the notion that it embodies a Messianic name, *'the Shoot,'* or *'the Sprout'* (נֵצֶר), which is found in Isaiah 11:1. The most likely suggestion is that it signifies *'Watch-tower'* (from נֹצְרָת). Aram נָצְרָה, נָצְרַת, a name which would be given first to the hill, and then to the town built on its flank. *Dictionary of the Apostolic Church,* vol. 2, James Hastings, John C. Lambert and John A. Selbie, eds., (Commentary by James Strahan professor of Hebrew, Magee College, Derry, 1915-1926), New York: Charles Scribner's Sons, 1918, p.79-80.
Retrieved from http:/archive.org/details/dictionaryofapos02hast
2. Matthew 2:23
3. John 19:19
4. Acts 22:8
5. Job 7:20 YLT
6. Acts 24:5
7. Luke 4:14
8. John 1:35-39
9. John 1:43
10. John 1:45-46
11. Acts 7:48
12. 1 Timothy 6:16
13. Mark 1:15

THE KINGDOM OF GOD
1. Romans 14:17
2. 1 Corinthians 4:20
3. Matthew 6:10
4. Luke 12:31
5. Mark 12:30
6. Matthew 11:12
7. 1 Peter 5:4
8. Luke 1:79

NOTES

9. Matthew 4:15
10. Mary Magdalene is Mary of the watchtower. *Magdala* is the Greek form of *migdol* and means tower, or watchtower. Smith, vol. 2, p.186-187. Retrieved from https://catalog.hathitrust.org/Record/007911777
11. Matthew 28:1

THE QUICKENING SPIRIT

IN THE IMAGE OF HIM
1. John 3:7 YLT
2. Colossians 3:9-10
3. Acts 6:1-6
4. Acts 7:55-56
5. Acts 6:5
6. Acts 6:8
7. Acts 6:10
8. Acts 6:11-14
9. Acts 7:1
10. Acts 7:54
11. 2 Corinthians 4:6
12. Acts 22:20
13. Galatians 1:15-17
14. 2 Corinthians 11:27
15. 1 Corinthians 2:14-16
16. Philippians 3:21

CELESTIAL BODIES
1. 1 Corinthians 15:44
2. Daniel 10:6
3. Luke 2:8-9
4. Matthew 28:2-3
5. Luke 24:1-10
6. John 20:27

NEITHER THE DAY NOR THE HOUR
1. Matthew 24:51
2. Judges 16:19-22
3. Judges 16:23-31

COMMANDING FAITH
1. Matthew 13:31-32
2. Luke 17:21

3. Ephesians 3:19
4. Matthew 18:3
5. Colossians 1:27
6. Luke 9:44
7. John 12:36
8. Revelation 22:13

SEEING INTO HEAVEN

HEAVENLY THINGS
1. John 10:3
2. Mark 1:35
3. 1 Corinthians 6:17
4. 1 John 2:8
5. 1 Thessalonians 5:17
6. Matthew 6:7
7. Matthew 26:38-44

THE STRUGGLE WITH SLEEP
1. Exodus 16:19-20
2. Luke 21:37; 22:39-40
3. John 16:33
4. Matthew 26:36-38
5. John 16:32

LIVING IN THE SPIRIT
1. 1 Corinthians 15:51-52
2. John 1:12

www.ingramcontent.com/pod-product-compliance
Lightning Source LLC
Chambersburg PA
CBHW041956080526
44588CB00021B/2764